# FOOD FOR GOD'S CHILDREN
## by Raphael Gasson

**LOGOS INTERNATIONAL**
Plainfield, New Jersey

All direct Scripture quotations
are from the King James Version,
unless otherwise indicated.

# Contents

# FOOD FOR GOD'S CHILDREN

# The Staple Diet of the Hebrews

It is an interesting study to trace modern conceptions of things backwards through the centuries, noting how often the same ideas, although perhaps in a different guise, and possibly not related in the same way, appear in the forefront of a nation's history.

This is particularly so in the case of food values and modern dietetics which have become, in comparatively recent years, such a matter of consideration to the mass of people in this country. Nowadays, it is taken for granted that, since a healthy body largely depends on the food with which it is supplied, it is a matter of great importance that the caterer or cook or consumer—preferably all three—should have an expert knowledge of the various values of different types of food. The application of this knowledge to the preparation and supply of food, avoids unnecessary eating of foodstuffs that have little or no value at all. This will lead to a careful choice and will result in sufficient care being taken with cooking so that the food will be nutritious, palatable and generally beneficial to the consumer.

Waste will be also eliminated from the household

budget—at least unnecessary waste—as each particle of food can be put to the use for which it is intended. It is surprising how little food becomes waste matter when one has a proper idea of the bodily value of the various foods that come to our tables.

Throughout the ages, the housewife has had to deal with the problem of supplying sufficient food to her family within the limited means at her disposal, both with regard to cash limitations and the seasonal supplies of food available. These were her main problems to cope with, yet little attention was paid, until later years, as to whether or not the food thus consumed was particularly good in the essentials for human health.

Strangely enough, health itself was not necessarily thought of in connection with food, and the few foods which were considered to be good for certain ailments were too often matters of superstition rather than of any exact knowledge of food values.

To turn as far back in history as the establishment of the Mosaic Law given to the Israelites, seems a very far cry from our present twentieth century; yet it is surprising to find that the part of this law which appertains to the eating, and abstinence from eating, of certain foods is, in its substance, very similar to modern views regarding things of valuable edibility.

The following classifications are an attempt to bring out this similarity. We must bear in mind that the law of Moses was literally the law of God given through Moses to His redeemed people. As such, it had a twofold purpose. Firstly, it served to maintain a correct relationship with the Lord God himself, and, secondly, it served to keep the people as healthy and free from contamination as was possible. The second purpose is, of course, part of the first, for great stress was laid on the people

2

being unblemished both spiritually and physically. As far as the priesthood and the animals used for sacrificial purposes were concerned, the idea was taken even further—for only unblemished men were allowed to become priests, and only unblemished animals were considered capable of being offered as sacrifices.

The Law, given to the Israelites with this in view, will repay any study that is given to it by richly rewarding one with a double-edged list of interesting items which can be applied both to the body and to the spirit. This is, of course, more than modern dieticians attempt to combine unless it is in their trend to accept the fact that a healthy body assists in the upkeep of a mind. However that may be, it is hoped that a fresh slant to the study may be given in the following pages, and that we may see the reason why such laws were made for such a people. It is further hoped that our study will be edifying, not only to see how the essentials of modern thought were laid down in the Mosaic Law, although the food values were not specifically stated as such—but to see how a parallel runs between the needs of the body and the needs of the spirit inasmuch as things to be avoided in one sphere are likewise to be avoided in the other.

One is inclined, on thinking it over, to agree with the preacher when he says that "there is no new thing under the sun" (Eccles. 1:9). Consequently, the pages of history bring up-to-date lessons for those who read them in this frame of mind.

Three main things are carried out by foods. Firstly, they serve to build up the tissues of the body and repair it; secondly, they provide heat and energy and, thirdly, they supply substances and vitamins which help to give fitness and vitality to the body and resistance to the different attacking diseases.

It is undoubtedly true that our physical health depends very largely on our diet which must have a balance of vitamins, proteins and carbohydrates. As an engine requires fuel in order to work properly, the body needs certain food elements to keep it in proper working order, and it demands that these elements should be supplied in correct proportions. It therefore stands to reason that if one of these food essentials is absent or given in the wrong proportion, illness will result. Therefore, it is important to plan correctly balanced meals. In order to plan such meals, it is necessary to have some knowledge of food classifications and their comparative food values.

Avoiding certain types of foods is vitally important to the planning of a proper diet. A heavy meal of flesh foods—with the usual starches, sugars and condiments that accompany it—tends to make controlled attention and concentration of the consumer difficult. He will have to make especially great efforts to attend to his work, because such a heavy meal envelops the eater with a kind of mental fog.

For this reason, the practice of fasting is valuable because it aids one's mental attention to a subject instead of dividing his attention periodically between the stomach and the brain.

In historical times, the typical Hebrew household maintained an almost exclusive vegetarian diet. The use of meat, although technically allowed by law, was not regarded as an absolute necessity to well-being, and the cost of it confined its use to special occasions such as family festivals or the visits of an honored guest.

To counteract this lack of meat, various cereals were used to make up the main part of the meal. These were generally classified as "corn." Wheat and barley were mainly used and were largely devoted to making household bread. In the case of the poorer classes, barley bread was the principal food as it was considerably cheaper.

Great use was made of different pulse foods and edible herbs.

4

## The Staple Diet of the Hebrews

Lentils and beans were in this category as they were easily obtainable and popular. They were probably eaten by Daniel (Dan. 1:12-16) and Jacob made his fateful meal of pottage with red lentils (Gen. 25:29-34). This type of stew in which the lentils are flavored with onions and other ingredients, is still very much in favor as a dish in Syria today.

It may be remembered that the Israelites, when wandering through the wilderness, looked back very wistfully to a time when they were able to feed on cucumbers, melons, onions and leeks as an addition to the flesh meat and fish which they enjoyed when they were living in the land of Egypt (Num. 11:5). These were, of course, unobtainable in the wilderness, although they were subsequently cultivated in Palestine to add variety to meals for those who could afford them.

Apart from these foods, it was usually possible to obtain figs and olives for consumption in their seasons, and most Jewish households maintained a well-kept vegetable garden and small fruit trees. It was the task of the housewife to keep these tended and to ensure that a sufficiency of fresh vegetables and fruit was at hand whenever necessary. As much as the ground would yield was demanded of it, while fish was occasionally brought inland and gladly used when the price was not prohibitive.

Consequently, the diet as a whole, supplemented with seasonal supplies of occasional imports, contained all that was necessary, from even the modern point of view, of body-building, energy-giving and disease-resisting elements, although the people were probably not conscious of this.

# 2

# Laws and Accusations Concerning Blood

From ancient times, even as far back as Josephus, the most senseless and untruthful charges have been leveled against Jews, accusing them of human sacrifices or of using human blood for the preparation of the unleavened bread as used in the Passover.

According to the biblical injunction, Jews were forbidden to partake of blood. There is also a good deal of ritual devoted to ensuring the scrupulous removal of all blood from meat before it is prepared for eating. This even includes the drawing of blood from the veins. Yet there has been a persistent spread of belief over the years that Jews have used blood in their ritual, and they have been accused of stealing children to murder for the sake of using their blood. Few charges against any religious groups have been as monstrous as those which have been made against the Jews; few have had such fatal results as these blood ritual charges and accusations. Popes have issued bulls; sultans have published denials; and many have protested. Yet, over the ages, Jews have been accused, tried and punished in spite of the fact that none of these purported crimes have been proved. In almost every place where Jews have settled, they have never been free from blood accusations.

In 1840, when Father Thomas, a Franciscan monk who was much respected by the Jews in Damascus, disappeared, a charge of ritual murder was brought against the Jewish community. Many were tortured into making a false confession, and a large number died under these tortures. Numerous Jews became victims of mass violence and synagogues were pillaged until foreign intervention and deputations resulted in exposing the absurdity of the accusation. Finally, Jewish prisoners were released and all subsequent attempts to reopen these charges failed—at least in Damascus.

These unsuccessful accusations in Damascus did not prevent similar charges elsewhere, for in 1882 there occurred a most extraordinary situation in Hungary. When a Christian peasant girl, named Esther Solymosi, failed to return to her village, the anti-Semitic leaders proposed that all Jews should be expelled following the rumor of ritual murder. Strangely enough, the main witness against the Jews was a five-year-old Jewish boy who was talked into accusing his own father, an officer of the synagogue. Following this, the mother and other members of the family were accused together with other Jews. Many were put to death, including a fourteen-year-old boy who was tortured into making a confession.

Oddly enough, a body of a girl was later found in the river Theiss and the mother identified her daughter's clothes but not the body itself which was buried very hastily. This resulted in a further charge being brought against the Jews that they must have found another body and clothed it with the clothes of Esther Solymosi in order to create a mystery. Many more arrests followed and proceedings dragged out for months. The defense eventually succeeded in ordering an exhumation of the body which, in spite of decay, was lacking any evidence of ritual

8

murder, yet it was established that the body was that of the missing girl.

In 1899, Agnes Hruze, a nineteen-year-old, was found murdered near Polna, Bohemia, and suspicion was leveled against twenty-three-year-old Leopold Hilsner, who was a Jewish vagrant. Although no evidence of an incriminatory nature was found against him, he was arrested and charged with ritual murder. He was easily frightened into a confession as well as naming two accomplices who were later able to establish that they were not at the scene of the crime at the time.

Hilsner was eventually convicted and sentenced to death, but an appeal was lodged. A fresh trial was ordered during which Hilsner first withdrew his confession and then repeated it, although his supposed accomplices had well-established alibis. A very bitter anti-Semitic agitation followed in Vienna which resulted in Hilsner being accused of a second crime. He was condemned and sentenced to death. This was commuted to a life sentence and then Hilsner was finally released. He eventually died at the age of fifty in Vienna.

In 1911, in Russia, Mendel Beilis was charged with the murder of a Christian child for the purpose of blood ritual. The proceedings were slow and torturous, dragging out over a number of years. The Russian government itself was a party to the accusation in its attempt to use the situation to add fuel to the fire and encourage a general anti-Semitic feeling. The matter, which strongly resembled the Dreyfus affair, had the participation of many important people, and the whole case was followed with great intensity and emotion in world Jewry.

Even before the body of the missing child was found, a great cry was made that Jews had committed the murder for ritualistic purposes. Then, when the badly gashed body was discovered, a drunken man and his wife both testified to having seen a black-bearded man, resembling Beilis, with the child. He was arrested and spent two years in prison while all attempts were made to find evidence linking him with the crime.

In an attempt to scientifically prove that the Jews used blood in their religious rites, the government enlisted Professor Sikorsky, an eminent neurologist, while other experts on Jewish matters were called in for the long trial. Significantly, the accused was hardly mentioned during the trial, which seemed to be more of an attempt to prove that Jews were responsible for blood rituals. Although the charge was supported by many prominent anti-Semitists, Beilis was completely cleared of the charge; but, broken in health after his long bitter struggle, he eventually died in the United States.

The distinction between clean and unclean foods was first introduced in the Sinaitic Legislation. However, the idea of the blood was no novelty for its use was expressly forbidden to Noah (Gen. 9:3-4), the blood being the life of the flesh. It is a deep-rooted belief in man to hold the blood of animals or humans as sacred. This is probably due to the idea that the blood is the life-giving fluid and the vital essence of existence, for the Hebrew word *nephesh* speaks of the significance of life being resident in the blood. Consequently, when a victim was slain, the blood which drained from the veins still held within it the very life of which it was the vehicle—the blood-soul. The idea suggests that the blood might be alive for some time after the body is dead and thus, by drinking it, there exists the possibility that the qualities of the victim could be acquired by the drinker. Underlying the whole prohibition regarding the drinking of it and the dread of physical pollution, is the fear that such pollution would automatically bar the safe access to God.

Yet the sacredness of blood can go even deeper when its efficiency as an atonement for sin is brought into the discussion; for the Word of God tells us that the blood is given "upon the altar to make an atonement for your souls" (Lev. 17:11). The conception of the power of atonement through the blood reaches its zenith in the institution of the Day of Atonement under the Mosaic Law whereby with the shedding of blood there is atonement for all conscious and even unconscious sins, as well as assurance of a perfect reconciliation with God, leading to a renewed and proper relationship with Him.

The injunction in the Word of God as to the availability of atonement through the blood presents little problem to present-day Jews, who will enter their synagogues and spend the Day of Atonement in prayer and fasting when, in fact, they have no such atonement since this can only be secured through the shedding of blood. Such early fundamentals are now ignored because the Talmud teaches that since the destruction of the temple, prayers and the study of the Torah amply compensate for the absence of the blood sacrifice. It is even more effective if such prayers and study are combined with good works and intention. Any Jew who is exercised in mind concerning the bloodless atonement would have rabbinical assurance that blood is no longer necessary since God can see the intentions of the heart. This is a true statement as far as God's discernment is concerned, yet how futile it is when we realize that the offering is even at the door in the nature of the blessed Son of God who not only became sin, but by His own blood became the sin offering. This accomplished our atonement and it becomes effective when we believe in His name.

Unaware of this atonement, the people will pray for it according to the traditions of men rather than by the way in which God has chosen and planned. They will then beat their chests and pray, "We have trespassed, we have been faithless, we have robbed, we have spoken basely, we have committed iniquity, we have wrought unrighteousness, we have been presumptuous, we have done violence, we have forged lies, we have counseled evil, we have spoken falsely, we have scoffed, we have revolted, we have blasphemed, we have been rebellious, we have acted perversely, we have transgressed, we have persecuted, we have been stiff-necked, we have done wickedly, we have corrupted ourselves, we have committed abomination, we have gone astray and we have led astray."

Following such a confession, they will pray to the God who knows the secrets of eternity and all mysteries, to grant pardon for all their iniquities, and remission of all their transgressions. What a tragedy that such efforts should be made in order to appease and find favor with a merciful and forgiving God. He is mindful of all our shortcomings, yet is ever ready to receive whoever calls upon the name of His Son and claims redemption through His death which is the only sacrifice made once and for all.

In spite of the many vain philosophical and ingenious speculations of modern scholars who may seek to destroy the doctrine of atonement, or even to modify it, the fact remains that Christ's self-sacrifice will never cease to be the essential basis of the gospel. This was the teaching of the early church and has always been the means of exposing and illustrating the dreadfulness and horror of sin which is a challenge and an affront to a holy God. Yet He meets that need at Calvary through the shed blood and reveals His mercies which are new every morning and which pass all knowledge and comprehension.

Up to the present day, the Jew has abstained from eating flesh which contains blood. To ensure this, the blood is drained before the meat is cooked. Although this rite is carried out solely because it is enjoined upon them to do so by religious laws, we can see, from a modern point of view, why these instructions were given in the first place.

## Laws and Accusations Concerning Blood

It is obvious that early Jews would have been ignorant of the reasons for such rigidity; but, in the light of present medical knowledge, we can see that the prohibition of blood is wrapped up in the knowledge of the circulatory system. From what we know of this subject today, it is obvious that the blood in a corpse would be impure, for it would not have been transmitted through the lungs for purification. Although this would apply only to half of the blood supply—the other half having gone through the process of purification and having been carried through the arteries instead of the veins—there would be a sufficient quantity of impure blood to render such meat dangerous if taken as flesh for food.

The consumption of animal tissues is restricted by Jewish law and there are many prohibitions concerning certain classes of animals. This will be discussed later. But abstention from blood is regarded as so important that it is felt necessary to ensure that the slaughtering of animals is carried out according to an approved standard.

The term *shehita* is applied to the slaughtering of animals for use as kosher, or pure, food. The basis of the ordinances of ritual slaughter is found in such scriptural injunctions as, ". . . then thou shalt kill of thy herd and of thy flock . . ." (Deut. 12:21). The oral law, such as the Talmud, the Tosefta and various codes, gives very exhaustive and rigid details governing the shehita. Many of these regulations are now in written form for constant reference and would need a great deal of consideration if dealt with in detail. Briefly, the shehita is performed by a well-trained and highly qualified, ordained slaughterer, the *shohet*. He has to be a man of good character, good health and he must be well-acquainted with the shehita laws and an expert on the conditions of the animals because he has to inspect them before and after slaughter.

Great stress is thus laid on the training of the shohet in every

13

detail, even to the sharpening of the knife which must not have any imperfections. The throat cutting, in order to produce rapid and painless loss of consciousness with complete blood drainage, must be effected with one stroke and without interruption. There must be no pressure with the flawless blade in order to ensure a quick and painless death.

A study of this method of slaughter has been carefully made by surgeons and scientists and it has been conceded to be the most humane method. It also renders the flesh most conducive for human consumption.

The prohibitions of eating flesh with the blood and eating animals which had been strangled were only rigidly observed by Jews; but the matter was given a very important place for discussion in the early church. We read in Acts 15 that when many Gentiles sought admission to the church, which had hitherto been confined to Hebrew Christians, a council was held in Jerusalem in order that a definite ruling might be reached concerning the keeping of the Mosaic Law. The law itself, as far as ceremonies are concerned, was considered to be outside of the Gentiles' responsibilities and of no concern to them; yet it was insisted that these believers should remain under the obligation to abstain from things strangled and therefore from blood. This automatically means that the law concerning blood pertains to both Jew and Gentile, and remains one of the adjuncts of the Christian faith—one of the "thou shalt nots" of the New Testament, very much disregarded by modern Christians even if "it seemed good to the Holy Ghost, and to us" (Acts 15:28).

Even if we disregard the religious aspect of the blood completely, it is still a very forceful health rule. If we would take sufficient trouble with the preparation of our foods to ensure that what we are eating is as pure as we know how to make it, this would engender a healthier body. We can rely on our Lord, who does all things well and is mindful of our physical and spiritual needs, to know that the injunction to abstain from blood must be of paramount importance. To know that we have thus made our food as conducive to good health as possible will add to our personal enjoyment of eating it. This will result in greater peace of mind and add to our general welfare.

# 3

# Dietary Laws
# of the Israelites

Although the study of diet may be thought of as a modern
subject, it is remarkable that these laws, given to the people of
Israel centuries ago, conform very much to modern ideas. They
were obviously far from being merely a set of difficult and
unnecessary laws given to keep the people occupied, but were
of the utmost value from the point of view of cleanliness and
purity. In addition to the hygienic aspect, they contain many
spiritual types which supply us with a unique law which is
profitable both to the body and to the spirit.

A very important set of rules in this law pertained to the
clean condition of all food eaten, and through the following of
these ordinances, the Hebrews were able to keep themselves
separate from other peoples. Food to be eaten by them had to
be technically clean, and anything that had even been touched
by a Gentile was regarded as unclean for it was thought possible
that the Gentile had impurity in his hands. For this reason they
abstained from beer and wine made from products grown in
Gentile vineyards.

The law imposed, among other things, that a kid was not to
be seethed in its mother's milk. This will be referred to later in

a more devotional sense, but here it will be useful to know that the teachers of the law explained to the people that the two would mix in the stomach and it is not considered correct to mix unnatural foods. Even today, Orthodox Jews abstain from mixing milk with meat at the same meal, and will even refuse milk for several hours after partaking of meat. On the other hand, it is permissible to eat meat only a short interval after drinking milk. This may seem somewhat inconsistent, but in the light of present-day knowledge of the fact that milk can digest in a shorter time than meat, we can understand why such a rule was imposed.

This prohibition of mixing meat and milk does not apply to the flesh of fish which may be cooked in milk and taken together, for such blending would not have harmful consequences.

After reading of the various food prohibitions, many people may be inclined to exaggerate the trouble or inconvenience caused by following these laws. However, in the interests of good health and peace of mind, this would not be any more irksome than to avoid eating cats and dogs.

The housewife would see to it that she had certain obligations in the preparation of food for the family and one of these is to ensure that it was clean. In this respect also, great attention would be paid to the washing of the hands before handling any kind of food. The rabbis spent considerable time discussing this aspect of cleanliness and personal hygiene, even to the extent of considering the correct method of hand-washing to be adopted by the mass of the people in order to ensure maximum safety in the maintenance of good health.

Much questioning arose as to how, and under what circumstances, the hands should be washed. Should the whole hand, or only part of it be immersed in water? Should the water cover the fingers or the whole hand as far as the wrists? Should the hands be held up or down? These questions may appear to be very fussy, yet we need to understand that there was an intense and godly desire to do what was right and God-honoring. Perhaps we as Christians could seek to uphold a greater Christ-honoring stance in our work and leisure. Too often the Christian who seeks to walk carefully is criticized for being overscrupulous, for adhering too closely to the Word of God and because he desires to live a Christ-centered life.

Doubtless, the decisions reached in the matter of hand-washing were the result of much anxiety and perplexity of soul. There would have been much prayer and fasting, much casting upon God and much dependence upon the guidance of the Holy Spirit in the anxious desire to offer nothing but the best to a holy and merciful God.

The ultimate decisions reached were that the hands should be submerged in water with the fingers pointing down to avoid any possible germs adhering to them or being washed up the arm instead of away from the body. By holding the fingers down, a more thorough cleansing would be achieved. In these days of modern water supplies, such cleansing would take place quite automatically when washing the hands under a running tap—a method often given preeminence by the medical profession—but when the Hebrew law was given, the Israelites obtained their water from wells, rivers and cisterns, and this necessitated special rulings to be drawn up in order to reduce to a minimum the possibility of infection.

Similar regulations applied to the cleansing of cooking utensils. There were metal and earthenware dishes, glass and possibly leather bottles, all of which required special rules. It became the rabbis' responsibility to establish and to make known the essential details in maintaining purity both in the preparation and in the eating of food. Possibly, where such preoccupation with minute details is carried out, there is a danger that the original intention of the law might be obscured. Also, in the course of time, so much attention could be paid to external things that the internal importance might become of secondary, instead of primary, importance. Many Christians are likewise overconcerned about their outward appearance, to the detriment of their spiritual development. Yet we should be particular with regard to the "whole" man, for the world often knows how a Christian should walk and many great sermons can be preached without a word being uttered. A Spirit-filled believer can reveal the Lord's beauty in his life even without the foolishness of preaching. How many fine sermons have been undermined by the preacher's own inconsistency? How often a godly person has been avoided in his own little fellowship because he is "too fussy" about his testimony.

Truly we know that the letter of the law can stifle or restrict, and carrying things out to the letter can kill; but if things are carried out in the right spirit and with a godly intention, led and strengthened by real Holy Spirit-power, we are set at liberty and made alive. The Word of God becomes, not a set of dead rules, but a living influence so that we desire to obey, and this obedience sets us at liberty. We obey, not because we are told to, but because we want to. As a simple example, we can think of the command of the Lord Jesus Christ to remember His death "till he come" (1 Cor. 11:26). This is done in simple obedience as we gather around the Lord's table and partake of the bread and wine. How often we may say in such a meeting, "Lord, we are here in simple obedience to your command." Very commendable, but supposing the Lord had not so commanded? Would we meet as such just the same because we have the intense desire to please Him? How delighted He could be, and what joy it would be to the heart of the blessed God if our breaking of bread service was carried out, not so much because He so commands, but because we love Him and know that it would please Him.

The Jewish dietary laws were not instituted consciously for hygienic reasons. Nevertheless, the sanitary and hygienic aspects are an essential basis for their scientific evaluation.

The Hebrew word *kasher* denotes food which, by virtue of its pure nature, is conducive to proper nourishment. *Terephah* conveys the idea of that which is unhealthy, toxic, inadequate for the need, or capable of causing an ill effect.

In subsequent chapters we shall be looking at clean and unclean creatures in an attempt to see what spiritual lessons we can learn from scriptural injunctions concerning them. Here it may be profitable to offer a digest of certain zoological features which may have some bearing on the question as well as help us to understand a little of certain theories belonging to the realm of evolution.

It is not the intention here that we should be taken up with speculative theories because we have something of greater import to consider. Nevertheless, evolutionary zoology does help us to see that more primitive animal organisms are less adapted to alimentary purposes than those of a more complex constitution. Hence, the various *Reptilia, Mollusca* and *Crustacea* are not in themselves sufficient for diet. Furthermore, their flesh can induce various forms of intoxication, for these lower forms of animal life are infected with a variety of microorganisms which have a weak power of resistance and very low vitality. The simpler the animal construction, the less fit it is for human consumption for it is too easily decomposed and more likely to create a number of physical and constitutional disturbances.

There are four species of locust which are permitted as food, but their exact nomenclature and identity is so involved and doubtful that it is very difficult to identify them.

The tortoise carries a number of organisms under its shell

while the turtle flesh has been found to be the cause of a number of deaths. Likewise, the snail, mussel and the different varieties of crab have the same harmful potential.

The Word of God forbids eating fish without fins and scales (Lev. 11:10). Again, evolutionary zoology teaches us that those with fins and scales, with the squamous tunics are of the higher type than those without, having a higher standing on the evolutionary ladder. Ignoring the theory of evolution, we will be able to see that fish with fins and scales are obviously cleaner, and it should be of no surprise that God, who knows all things and does all things well, should ensure that Moses was able to write these laws as he was led by the Holy Spirit to do so.

Another fact, often mentioned in hygiene textbooks, is the danger of communicability of typhoid through eating the oyster. The eel is also difficult to digest.

The evolution zoologist will further tell us that primordial organisms have almost all subsisted on a flesh or protoplasm-devouring regimen, and that they have acquired a tendency to subsist on a vegetable diet. We know that animals which depend on vegetables for their nutrition possess delicate and tender muscular fibers which demand little effort in digestion.

The flesh of the rodents is hard to digest and is prohibited. Because of its filthy habitat, the swine is one of the most dangerous animals to eat. Trichinosis attacks the swine. Its intestines can become infested with the *taenia solium* and the *taenia mediocanell* (types of tapeworm) as well as other parasites. These can be of great danger to the partaker.

As domestic fowls exhibit delicate muscular fibers, they are more savory and digestible than the wild duck and other birds such as are pronounced to be unfit for consumption.

One of the potent sources of tuberculosis was discovered in

the meat of consumptive animals, and it was in 1934 that an inspection of meat and milk revealed that the Jewish system of slaughter and hygiene was not only the most painstaking but was the most efficient. In this system adequate steps are taken, not only to maintain purity at the slaughter stage, but to prevent any infected meat from reaching the family table.

This is a vindication, not only of the Jewish method of slaughter, but of the Word of God which was able to make plain what was fit for human consumption before any theories of evolution were considered. The Word also declares that cattle which have perished from disease must not be eaten, because as soon as an animal succumbs to disease it can become a harboring place of numerous lower and harmful forms of life.

The meat that reaches the Jewish table is fresh, clean, wholesome and free from pathogenic organisms. In short, it is kosher.

We can marvel at the profound wisdom of the Bible as it tells us all that is necessary for our salvation, leading to a sanctified and wholesome enjoyment and appreciation of what God has done. Here we see not only divine wisdom, for we can see that our heavenly Father, in great mercy, has given us ordinances which aim at prevention rather than cure. Here we have a wonderful set of divine precepts, which not only apply to the distant past of the Mosaic Law, but are up-to-date and in accord with the doctrines of modern sanitation. Here we have divine regulations which are, interestingly enough, backed up by the anti-God evolutionist and are compatible with all that modern hygiene dictates.

So the Word of God is the pioneer of all the sanitary sciences of our present day.

# 4

# God's Provision for the World

The fact that it is necessary for creatures to take food stresses the fact that man is fully dependent on God's provision, for we are told in the Word that it is in "him we live, and move, and have our being" (Acts 17:28). We live only by Him, are sustained by Him and are nourished by His bountiful supply. Nevertheless, while we readily agree that food is an essential physical need, we must also acknowledge that the same is equally true in the case of our spiritual need, for we read that "Man shall not live by bread alone, but by every word that proceedeth out of the mouth of God" (Matt. 4:4).

From both the physical and spiritual aspects we find that the very necessity for proper nourishment reveals a proper position of dependence upon God, and one important fact which is constantly brought to our attention is that our whole physical and spiritual constitution can be strengthened or weakened by the food we allow to become part of us.

In Genesis 1:11-13, after God had restored order out of a scene which was without form and void, He caused the dry land to appear on the third day and we have the "herb yielding seed, and the fruit tree yielding fruit after his kind, whose seed is in itself." There is something really living about a seed, so small, yet possessing such potentiality, for this seed could have the inward power to produce a forest which could cover the earth.

We can thus see how important it is that the food we have must have the life-giving power within it; such fruit-producing seed must contain the vital elements which are marked by the power of reproduction. The Lord could say, "I have meat to eat that ye know not of" (John 4:32), and again, "I live by the Father: so he that eateth me, even he shall live by me" (John 6:57). Is there a principle of life in the kind of food we are allowing to form our constitution? If there is not, we should avoid it and seek out the right kind of seed which is going to be reproductive. Even the beasts have "every green herb." They are green because they are fresh and full of sap. Thus, if we want spiritual freshness and vitality we must ensure that we have fresh and life-giving food.

Later, in Genesis 1:29, we are told that this was God's provision for man, as if to say that God would have us to feed on nothing other than what He has provided. When our minds and affections need feeding and developing in a spiritual way, nothing but what is of Christ will sustain us.

Unfortunately, many believers suffer much harm in their spiritual constitutions by appropriating the wrong kind of food, for there are so many elements in the world that destroy their spiritual appetites.

It was God's thought that man should share of the tree of life, but Satan caused Eve to take of the fruit of the tree of the knowledge of good and evil in defiance of God's command. This resulted in the Fall of Man and the fall of the whole creation. The Word of God gives us a very solemn warning that we could be spared much sorrow if we gave more diligence to the source of our food supply. If we merely feed our desires and tastes, which mark us as fallen creatures, we only strengthen those desires and lose our spiritual happiness.

The enemy would naturally suggest that certain things will do us no harm, that they are much to be desired, until we discover that there are those attractive things which do not develop within us what is of Christ. The end result is much agony and distress of soul and separation from God.

After the flood God provided man with "every moving thing that liveth" (Gen. 9:3) in addition to the previous provisions. But the blood, being God's reserve, was not to be taken, as if to remind us of that perfect redemption through the blood of Christ—the shedding of blood being God's final prerogative. He would constantly remind us by our daily food that everything for our pleasure is based upon His excellency expressed at Calvary. It is by faith in the excellency of the Lord's death that we are found to be acceptable. He had to die and rise again to make this possible, and the blood speaks of God's love, for the Lord himself said that He laid down His life that He might take it up again; no man could take it from Him, for He took it up again in resurrection (John 10:17-18).

Genesis 27 is a very sorrowful chapter for it reveals the tragic results of failing to see the truth of such a principle. We see the low state into which even men of faith can sink due to such lack of perception, so that it is possible to be a true saint without being able to form a clear judgment which would enable one to refuse his natural tastes. The condition of weakness can be overcome if we are prepared to walk in the line of God's will. There is no need for us to be spiritually weak for there is available a full provision for our strength and we can draw upon infinite resources in Christ (Eph. 6:10). Thrown back on his own resources and natural tastes, Isaac came under the influence of the wrong man for he loved Esau because he brought back venison which was "to his taste." Such a carnal appetite now develops into "savoury meat, such as I love"

(Gen. 27:4) so that Isaac is ready to entangle the purpose and promise of God in order to satisfy himself.

The venison might be eaten, by the law of Moses, but it could not be used for sacrifice. This possibly hints of the level on which Isaac lived. There was nothing particularly unclean in his standard of life—indeed, Esau's sin was a great grief to Isaac. Yet there was nothing sacrificial, no dedication to God's will. So, while we may question Rebekah's motive and method, she is seen in contrast to Isaac in that she could send Jacob to the flock to fetch an animal which is acceptable to God, for it is a picture of "the Lamb of God, which taketh away the sin of the world" (John 1:29).

Finally, we come to Joseph's administration in Egypt, and the word is "Go unto Joseph; what he saith to you, do" (Gen. 41:55).

Hopelessness and despair accompany the sinner wherever he goes; but there is bread in Egypt because Joseph is there and he has it stored up for those who go to him. Likewise, there is a sufficiency of bread available, even in this Christ-rejecting world, because Christ is found by all who seek Him and ask for Him in our time of spiritual famine. By realizing our need, we look to the future and call upon the name of the Lord. Many do this in time of extremity, in response to the word, "Go to Joseph" and the Holy Spirit, through the Word, continually points men to Jesus, the Christ. His teaching in the gospels is expounded by men of God. The New Testament explains the way of salvation. The Lord Jesus, like Joseph, opens up the storehouses of God's grace to supply our every need. He says, "Come unto me, all ye that labour and are heavy laden" (Matt. 11:28).

Those who went to buy corn were asked for money; but the water of life is given to us freely. Thank God for the sense of famine which drives us to find satisfaction in the Lord Jesus.

## God's Provision for the World

If we long for food, it is only obtained in a place of Christ's administration and where we meet under His authority. There we have the blessings which He longs to give His own, for, when we are prepared to submit to His scriptural principles, we will find abundance of supply through our true Joseph. We can thus anticipate all the future enjoyment that awaits those who love Him and who pursue the path of separation from the principles of the world.

# 5

# Food in the Wilderness

In the same way that the supply of food was dependent on God's provision in the references cited from Genesis, we must find the source of our spiritual food in God.

When we come to the Book of Exodus, chapters 12 and 16, we find plenty of provision even in a very limited setting.

In chapter 12, there is abundance, and each head of every house was to take a lamb. Although they were under bitter bondage and seemingly without any resources, they had the right kind of provision in spite of what might appear to be abject poverty. God would have His own to be fed on such suitable food as would be sufficient to maintain them in their exodus from Egypt and during their wilderness experience. Here, the word to Pharaoh is, "Let my people go that they may serve me" (Exod. 7:16), for God will have a people who are not only redeemed from the world, as typified by Egypt, but a people who are nourished in the pilgrim way with proper food.

This applies to us in our present time. Only those who can depart from worldliness in the strength of the Holy Spirit will be able to be available for service in the midst of suffering. If we leave the world as it says in 1 Peter 4:1-2, it may well involve

31

suffering.

The Passover is such an important institution that we should desire to realize its full significance. It draws us to thoughts of the suffering Savior and gives us a clear impression of Him who bears the sins of the world. It could not be said that Israel was any better than Egypt, but we do learn that there is only one ground on which a holy God can have a people fit to serve Him. That ground is Christ whose precious blood satisfies every holy claim with regard to our sins. How can we continue in sin, or enjoy fellowship with evil after eating the Passover and seeing His holy sufferings, which stand as a shelter from the judgment of a righteous God?

We note, for the first time, the mention of such expressions as "all the assembly of Israel" and "the whole assembly of the congregation of Israel" (Exod. 12:6), and we learn that such an assembly was composed of households. It is blessed to think of tens of thousands of households where Christ is known as our Passover Lamb.

From the outset, it was in the mind of God that His people should be closely knit together to form one body. Unfortunately, many Christians seek independent ground and find themselves without the authority of the church. But in Exodus we see that all partook of the Passover Lamb and celebrated the Feast of Unleavened Bread. For this they had to subject their own individuality to the assembly of the people, and God in His providence gave them help. He would act the same today if we would also be willing to come under His authority, for it is necessary that we should learn of His righteousness and favor which brought about our redemption. We have to acknowledge that we are not morally better than those of the world, any more than the Israelites were better than the Egyptians. We are not more able than the Egyptians or the world to stand naturally in the presence of a God who can judge in all righteousness. We find that there is only one ground on which we can claim deliverance and that is God's mercy through Christ himself who bore in His own body the judgment of God. His death and the shedding of His precious blood gave perfect satisfaction to every requirement of God and He must have a people who can recognize this truth.

The lamb was to be a yearling, fully developed and with all the energy that speaks of Christ in His manhood and maturity. It was to be kept in the household for four days so that every heart and mind would be affected by the knowledge of its death for redemption. The thought of God is toward households as well as individuals. The command is "a lamb for a house" and we need to realize that nothing is gained by refusing to bow to this. Truly, our salvation is an individual matter, for it is a personal transaction with God through the death of His beloved Son. But we stand to lose some of the enjoyment and the gain of our own personal salvation if we overindividualize this and miss the conception that there must be households where the Lord Jesus Christ is known and fed upon, based on the principle that "thou shalt be saved, and *thy house*" (Acts 16:31, italics mine).

All aspects of the Passover and the Feast of Unleavened Bread had to have the characteristics of a household just as are found in every Orthodox Jewish home today. These same attributes should be evidenced in every Christian home where the Lord's name is upheld, where His death is seen and testified of with thankfulness. Thus, in each house, He can become the subject of our adoration as we view Him with unblemished perfection and spotlessness.

The Passover Lamb, kept for four days in the household, would affect every heart and mind by the knowledge of its death for each family member's redemption. As we view this, we see it in much detail in the gospels for we are shown how He endured the bitterness, desertion and wickedness of man in those four days before His death.

The lamb was to be eaten, as we are to feed on Christ who died for our sins. We find the bitter herbs which not only speak of the bondage of Egypt but of self-judgment, so that we may have fellowship with Him in His sufferings as He faced the whole sin question once and for all on the cross. We can never really enter into the very depths of those sufferings as they are more than can be uttered and are beyond our human comprehension. But our hearts should be profoundly moved as we contemplate the awfulness of sin and its horrific consequences, as we come to understand in some measure that it was our sins which were involved when He bore that judgment. That very cry of abandonment from the cross is intended to affect us and draw appreciation from our hearts. "Oh, what am I that I should be the object of God's wondrous grace? That He should send His Son to me, that I might see Him face to face? It was for me, for me He left His throne above; His grace, His goodness all for me; for me the ocean of His love" (J. L. Harding, "It Was for Me").

The staff was to be in their hands as they ate the Passover and they were to have their shoes on their feet because they were taking a journey out of Egypt into the wilderness, to a place where they could serve God. The Passover is just as applicable today as it was in the land and the wilderness, for we are called to the service of God. In this service, we take our journey from the world to the place where He has called us. Yet many of us find it possible to cling to the world and all its links while still putting our trust in the blood of Christ (Rom. 3:25) which shelters us from the judgment of God.

According to Luke 22:1, "the feast of unleavened bread" is called the Passover. Indeed, it lasted for seven days, and speaks of decrease. John the Baptist illustrated this when he said, "He must increase, but I must decrease" (John 3:30). He was prepared to go out of the public eye because he was satisfied and filled with the love of the Lord. When we are prepared to decrease, to get out of sight, sink our own importance and reduce ourselves in our own estimation, God will give us a greater impression of His Son. When we are prepared to leave our Egypt with its leeks and fleshpots, we will find ourselves nourished by a new and more satisfying kind of spiritual food, which will enable us to arrive at sound and spiritual judgments against those things which hinder our relationship with God himself and our fellowship with His people.

We need to "purge out therefore the old leaven, that ye may be a new lump, as ye are unleavened. For even Christ our passover is sacrificed for us" (1 Cor. 5:7). This "old leaven" belongs to the past while the unleavened bread of sincerity and truth is only to be found in the company of those who have partaken of the passover. What an exercise this is—not at all easy—but if we were anxious to be what God wants us to be it could have wonderful results. We are often in danger of trying to keep up worldly appearances without really being what we seem to others; but when the Lord comes in, things are different and we feed on Him as having died for our sins. We come under His rule and find ourselves linked with a people who are moving in the same direction to a different world—a divine inheritance. Here we all do the same thing, speak the same language and use such expressions as "blessed Lord Jesus," "praise His name," and "wonderful Savior"—a vocabulary unknown to those who are unregenerate. Here we make a public stand in confessing the Lord's name just as the people left Egypt in the sight of the Egyptians. They marched out of the land, denouncing all association with it. So we have a responsible position to maintain, and the more we meditate upon the lamb and all that it implies about the Lord's sufferings, the more we shall find ourselves separated from the world and feeding on unleavened bread. Then we shall be able to pour contempt on all our pride.

The Feasts of Passover and Unleavened Bread show us, in a typical way, that the world is judged, but in Exodus 16 we have an introduction to manna as a means to provide sustenance in the wilderness.

Manna means, "What is it?" The manna was unique for it could not be named or described in ordinary language. This is the same with the unique Jesus as represented here. He is God's "unspeakable gift" (2 Cor. 9:15) and He has a name that no one knows but himself (Rev. 19:12). He could say, "All things are delivered unto me of my Father: and no man knoweth the Son, but the Father; neither knoweth any man the Father, save the Son, and he to whomsoever the Son will reveal him" (Matt. 11:27).

Manna "was like coriander seed" (Exod. 16:31) for it cannot be compared with anything else. Similarly, the Savior, the seed or source of all things that exist, is incomparable, for "All things were made by him; and without him was not any thing made that was made" (John 1:3).

Manna was white, being a true description of the Savior. He is white with all the holiness and purity of the Godhead. "In him is no darkness at all" (1 John 1:5). Thus the manna had the characteristics of the deity of Christ and to taste of it was a wonderfully satisfying experience.

> But what to those who find? Ah, this
> Nor tongue nor pen can show;
> The love of Jesus, what it is
> None but His loved ones know.
> (Edward Caswall, "Jesus, the Very Thought of Thee")

## Food in the Wilderness

The supplying of the manna was indeed a great miracle. God was also teaching that "Man shall not live by bread alone, but by every word that proceedeth out of the mouth of God" (Matt. 4:4). It was a miraculous supply of a wonderful seed at a time of marvelous need; and it should deepen our sense of wonder at the works of God when we know that manna is still found in the desert or in the world. God's bread and water can never fail! Let us not think that when we leave Egypt and shake off the fetters of bondage that weaken and degrade, that He will leave us starving in a spiritual wilderness. As we struggle in our work to live honestly and bravely, as we fling off the habits which reign in the Goshen of commercial wealth and splendor, let us remember that our bread and water is sure. Let us learn a lesson from the history of Israel.

Now we need energy because the manna has to be gathered in the morning and before the heat of the day. We may grow apathetic or even lethargic so that we miss the necessary portion of nourishment and power of the Holy Spirit to strengthen us when the heat of the day brings its testings and trials.

Scripture describes the taste of the manna as being like "cake and honey" (Exod. 16:31), and there is the same lovely sweetness about the Lord Jesus as compared to the world which offers many inducements. These are offered from our youth upward and we have every opportunity of giving in to our natural longings.

We may not go back into the world in a physical sense; but we can go back mentally as the people did when they longed for Egypt in the wilderness. But how attractive is a heart which is satisfied by feeding on the things of Christ as characterized in the manna. In Matthew 11 we find an invitation to come to Him for He gives us rest when we take His yoke upon us.

The manna is seen again in the Revelation as the "hidden

manna" (2:17). It is in the golden pot and is the portion of the overcomer in Pergamos. Such a person would be continually feeding on the daily manna in the midst of much weakness and fragmentation among the Lord's people.

How we need these overcomers today in the face of Satan's subtle oppositions and deceptions. How the Lord would value such today and mark out those who are deserving of His special approval.

May our hearts be prepared to feed more on the spiritual nourishment of Christ so that our constitutions may be built up in order that we may be enabled to continue rendering a living testimony in our present wilderness position. May we be found faithfully serving Him until the day of His return.

# 6

# Food for a Holy People

The Book of Leviticus is a remarkable guide for it not only gives instruction as to the spiritual discernment which the saints need in order to distinguish between clean and unclean foods, but it gives clear and precise teaching as to the food necessary for the priests. In Old Testament days, the priests had a very important position in the mind of God for they would speak to us as having the true sensibilities and intelligence in their approach to the Throne of Grace.

God delights in the happy response of His people to himself and He would instruct us with a view to developing our spiritual power to respond to Him.

In chapter 2 we have teaching on the oblation which was of fine white flour and represented righteousness. It would be made into cakes and wafers and would be subjected to various forms of baking, representing different forms of testing to which the Lord Jesus was subjected in His path of service here. Thus, when He offered himself to God, He offered a life of perfect righteousness created by the experiences that He passed through in the flesh.

When the oblation was offered, the priest took his handful as a kind of first fruit and divided the offering into two parts representing the Godward side of the sacrifice of Christ and the side which reveals His love toward people. Some of the oil went with the handful, because it was by the power of the Holy Spirit that He offered himself to God.

The more we consider the pathway of the Lord Jesus, the more our hearts are affected by His perfection in humanity. In all the circumstances through which He passed, there were trials and testings, yet He remained constant as seen in the feature of fine flour. In His life there was nothing uneven, for in all His words and ways He pursued the path of His Father's will. Every test He endured brought out fineness as of flour so that even when He was faced with the most grieving of circumstances, He remained unchanged by them. He was never at a disadvantage, but humbly accepted every trial as having come from the very hand of His Father, for He had come to do God's will.

We also see the Lord's humanity characterized in the oblation, "baken in a pan" (Lev. 2:5), which was the instrument of heat. The pan, or oven (machabath), is seen in Ezekiel 4:3, as representing the enemies' artillery during the siege of Jerusalem. The pan was placed in position by the prophet to illustrate the forces of the enemy. Our own offering, the Lord Jesus himself, was also "baken in a 'pan' " of His enemies' hatred when the time came for Him to make that sacrifice.

The fine flour was "mingled with oil" as well as anointed with oil. This is a reference to the wonderful fact that the Holy Spirit had an important part in Christ's coming into manhood. As Luke tells us, "The Holy Ghost shall come upon thee, and the power of the Highest shall overshadow thee: therefore also that holy thing which shall be born of thee shall be called the Son of God" (1:35). John's Gospel unfolds the greatness of His person in saying, "The Word was made flesh, and dwelt among us"

(1:14). It was His own act and His humanity was unique, perfect and holy.

Then we have the offering of the first fruits, as another symbol of Christ himself, referring to the two wave loaves (Lev. 23:17), baked with leaven but not offered on the altar. This offering was looking to Pentecost, and viewing the saints as being filled with the Holy Spirit and forming part of God's great harvest as the fruit of Christ's death.

We should, therefore, seek for the power of the Holy Spirit in order that our own hearts may have deeper thoughts of Christ himself.

In the Books of Leviticus and Deuteronomy we are provided with a list of creatures which may or may not be eaten and, to further our study, it will be profitable to spend the rest of this section, and the six following, giving consideration to Leviticus 11.

The keynote of Leviticus 11 is found in verses 44-45: "For I am the LORD your God: ye shall therefore sanctify yourselves, and ye shall be holy; for I am holy: neither shall ye defile yourselves with any manner of creeping thing that creepeth upon the earth. For I am the LORD that bringeth you up out of the land of Egypt, to be your God: ye shall therefore be holy, for I am holy."

Here we have the fundamental reason for our sanctification and holiness, for we are to be holy in order that we may enjoy the relationship which God has granted to us with himself. Such sanctification involves a complete consecration to the service of God in which we are commanded to be holy because God himself is holy. If He is holy, His child must be holy for God is our Father and we must be like Him. Such holiness expresses an eternal hatred of sin and its consequences. God's choice of right and wrong are unchangeable. He is the only arbiter of right and wrong and without Him no standards have

41

meaning.

Furthermore, the instructions given here are based on the fact that the people were to be seen as "the children of the LORD your God" (Deut. 14:1). We should, therefore, take the instructions of Leviticus 11 and Deuteronomy 14 as a whole and understand that the important instructions in these two chapters are given in order that we should allow nothing to interfere with the perfect relationship which is established between the Lord God himself and His people.

The people of Israel were to realize that in keeping God's laws they would find in them a personal aid to holiness and, in this way, they would be fulfilling the purpose for which God had created man. Consequently, the mere fact of avoiding those foods which are termed unclean would be of actual physical and spiritual benefit, for bad food will result in an unhealthy body. Likewise, if we fail to fulfill the correct relationship with God by lack of spiritual sustenance, we will also have unhealthy souls.

Our Lord does not, however, merely order us to be holy and leave us to figure out for ourselves how to reach such a standard, but He goes to great lengths in order to show how a practical standard of holiness can be reached. How often we hear preachers exhorting their congregations to be holy. How often we are convicted of the need for a closer and more dedicated walk with God and the need to be filled with the desire for holiness. In the Word of God we have instructions on being holy which were worked out by almighty God for our benefit. In following the divine textbook we have a guide as to how we can find here a set of guidelines that will help us to ensure that nothing will interfere with our personal relationship with our holy God, or our own practical holiness.

We have already seen that the people were instructed to be careful not to eat anything that was unclean in order to maintain the correct standard of fitness so that they might give to God of their best in a physical sense. In the same light, it is obviously essential to take care what spiritual food is taken in from books, teachers and doctrines. If we are not holy within and without, we will not be able to enjoy God in all His fulness and we will not be in the desired spiritual state or condition to answer to His pleasure. Our relationship with God is twofold: "I will be to him a Father, and he shall be to me a Son" (Heb. 1:5). In other words, if we have God in any practical sense, it is because He has us; if He is to be our portion, we must be His portion also. We can only enjoy God properly when He enjoys us and if we wish to find satisfaction and pleasure in Him, this will only be possible if He can look on us and "see of the travail of his soul, and shall be satisfied" (Isa. 53:11). He will thus find pleasure in us. Does not this remind us that "We love him, because he first loved us" (1 John 4:19)? When we are feeding on those things that are unclean, a division is caused between the Lord and us and we will not be able to enjoy Him for He is a holy God. Unless we are prepared to allow the Holy Spirit to show us how to discern the distinction between things clean and unclean He will not find that joy and pleasure that He so desires to find in us and is ever ready to partake with us.

So what is greatly needful is an intelligent and spiritual discernment; but this must be by God's standards and not our own. It is only when we allow ourselves to be guided by the revelation of God through His written Word that we can ever hope to reach His standard of holiness.

Holiness is a very high standard, but the Spirit-filled believer should not desire it in any other way, for we should enjoy being taught how to discriminate between the clean and the unclean, the true and the false. We should also enjoy being taught how to refuse those things which do not suit God's holiness.

Let us not think that there are no moral standards in the world. Much has been done for good by great thinkers, philosophers and social reformers in history. Even Egypt had its moral codes which were commendable; but the children of Israel had been delivered and brought out of the land and chosen to be a separate and peculiar people unto God. They had been divinely elevated to such a relationship that it was imperative that they should realize the difference between the moral codes of man and the laws of God. The moral codes of many ordinary people, although good in themselves by worldly standards, are never good enough for God. He is the one who could pour plagues upon the Egyptians and bring about a mighty deliverance against the armies of Pharaoh, and could lead the people of Israel safely across the Red Sea so that these very people could enter a new existence. Similarly, the born-again Christian is a new creature in Christ, possessing a new position and all its consequences and this demands a new administration, new ideals, new experiences and new opportunities. All this entails greater repsonsibilities!

In the believer's position of grace, we know that all things are passed away and we have access to the Throne of Grace from which we would have been hopelessly lost and rejected. How much more, therefore, should we who have the Holy Spirit be stirring to attain the practical standard of personal holiness which is pleasing to a holy God? Under the power of God and through the guidance of the Holy Spirit we can thus be equipped to act according to the Word of God so that nothing should interfere in the holy relationship which we have with our Lord himself.

In Leviticus, chapter 10, verses 10-11, we read that the priests were instructed to "put difference between holy and unholy, and between unclean and clean." They were also instructed to "teach the children of Israel all the statutes which the LORD hath spoken unto them by the hand of Moses." If we cannot discern such things we cannot teach them and the first requisite of an aspiring teacher is that he should be teachable and taught of God.

We are called to a holy priesthood apart from the world, entering into a spiritual realm which has everything to do with the operations of the Holy Spirit. In this setting, we are not dependent on religious excitement and such influences which merely satisfy our natural sensibilities. If we are to preserve those spiritual conditions which are proper to the children of God who are called unto holiness, there is much to be avoided for it is sadly possible to lose our spiritual discernment. We need to take heed that we do not find ourselves offering "strange fire before the LORD, which he commanded them not" (Lev. 10:1), as did Nadab and Abihu who sinned while under the wrong influence.

Nevertheless there are certain things which excite the natural drives yet do not do violence to the natural conscience which may be unenlightened. We find it essential to seek instruction regarding such subtleties so that we may beware of them, to shun them if we are to keep ourselves in the proper condition of a holy priesthood.

The knowledge of such differences applies in every circumstance and at all times. In obedience to the Word of God, the people were to teach His instructions diligently to their children when they sit down and when they rise up (Deut. 6:7); this is a great lesson for Christians today for the world is full of those influences which are unholy, false and unclean. We have to ensure that we do not come into contact with them, for in doing so we can mar our personal relationship with God who has called us to be a holy people unto himself.

The eleventh chapter of Leviticus needs to be taken as a whole, and in so doing there are two very vital considerations which we, who are children of God, should bear in mind. They concern eating and touching.

Eating typifies those things which we take in and allow to become part of our own constitution. Some foods can be beneficial to our physical well-being while others are dangerous. In the spiritual sense we know that there are those things which hold a certain place in our hearts and minds. These can take the form of certain books we read and which we allow to form our spiritual constitution. Then there are those things which we listen to with great interest and with such intent that we put them before the revelation of God which is available to every believer through the Holy Spirit and the Word of God.

As we look around, we find that the world has much to offer in the way of literature; but sadly, much of this literature can be unclean because it concerns many of the base things of life. Much of it is unholy and false, able to lead the unwary from God so that even born-again believers can be lured from the truth revealed in the holy Scriptures, because they have paid more attention to what books and commentaries say about the Bible rather than what the Bible itself has to say. How easy it is to test a believer's spiritual stature by the kind of books exhibited in his bookcase. Unless our literature (even religious literature) is read in the light of God's Word, we build on a weak foundation which will only crumble and lead us to disaster, so that the final state will be worse than the beginning. May the Holy Spirit become so real to us that we have no desire to take in the things that are in opposition to what the Word of God has to say. If we take in such destructive literature and live by the standards which it advocates, we cannot be sanctified to the service of God, even though those standards may appear highly ethical. Any other way but God's way will only take us away from the truth, for we are solemnly warned that "There is a way which

46

seemeth right unto a man, but the end thereof are the ways of death" (Prov. 14:12).

Bearing in mind the twofold thought behind the dietary laws (eating and touching), eating is a very serious matter as our physical constitution depends on the proper nourishment. In the same way, we need to take scrupulous care with our spiritual food in order to maintain that peculiar relationship which has been provided for man with God through Calvary.

At a time such as we are living in today, we are anticipating the near return of the Lord when He will gather the church to himself. In these latter days, while we are looking for the blessed hope, we should seek to cherish our unique spiritual relationship and realize that there is a deep lesson to be learned from these instructions given to the Israelites. It is not difficult to see that these laws literally fulfilled the needs of a people who paid little attention, as far as we know, to the make-up of their diet, but who avoided the bad and partook of the good automatically because it was a law that just had to be obeyed. This same basic principle applies today both from a natural and a spiritual point of view. It was implanted in the minds of the Israelites, as a result of the rigidity of the law, that they could only enjoy their relationship with God in accordance with His will and to His entire satisfaction, while they strove to keep the law to the letter.

Could we not emulate the people of Israel? How much more should we who are living in the power of the Spirit be striving to live the laws of God in our own hearts? Should it not be our desire to raise our standards to such that will bring credit to the Lord rather than dishonor? Surely this will only be possible if we keep the law in our hearts; not because it is written but because it pleases God.

When we consider the second part of our twofold thought behind the dietary laws (that of touching), we know that touching also renders one unclean. This can happen without eating. Paul considers the same principle when he exhorts us to "come out from among them, and be ye separate, saith the Lord, and touch not the unclean thing; and I will receive you, and will be a Father unto you, and ye shall be my sons and daughters, saith the Lord Almighty" (2 Cor. 6:17-18).

Bearing in mind the implications of these chapters, let us take them as our divine guidebook as to what is clean and unclean. How gracious our Lord is to His own that, in commanding them to be a holy people, He should provide us with a set of divine rules which will aid us, testing and proving that which should occupy our thoughts and energies. It is His desire that we should be a people who can distinguish between good and evil, and this is only possible when we are prepared to trust in the guidance of the Holy Spirit and hold fast to the whole Word of God, rightly divided. When we are standing on the Word of God, we are on safe ground. If any doctrine goes against the things written therein it is because it is false and unclean, and anyone who proclaims it does so because he has no light.

God wants a people who can readily tell the difference between good and evil, clean and unclean, the true and the false. He has not only provided us with the Word of God as a guidebook, and the Holy Spirit to lead us into the truth, but He has given a perfect example of true purity and holiness in His beloved Son in whose steps we should ever strive to walk. Let us therefore follow God's instructions as to how to be holy, as we seek to witness for Him in this Christ-rejecting world.

# 7

# The Beasts
# of the Earth

"And the LORD spake unto Moses and to Aaron, saying unto them, Speak unto the children of Israel, saying, These are the beasts which ye shall eat among all the beasts that are on the earth. Whatsoever parteth the hoof, and is cloven-footed, and cheweth the cud, among the beasts, that shall ye eat. Nevertheless these shall ye not eat of them that chew the cud, or of them that divide the hoof: as the camel, because he cheweth the cud, but divideth not the hoof; he is unclean unto you. And the coney, because he cheweth the cud, but divideth not the hoof; he is unclean unto you. And the hare, because he cheweth the cud, but divideth not the hoof; he is unclean unto you. And the swine, though he divide the hoof, and be clovenfooted, yet he cheweth not the cud; he is unclean to you. Of their flesh shall ye not eat, and their carcase shall ye not touch; they are unclean to you" (Lev. 11:1-8).

We come to a very important feature of discernment in the Books of Leviticus and Deuteronomy and these first eight verses of Leviticus 11 indicate to us that we are to make a difference between the unclean and the clean. Here we are shown how to make this difference and it is most important that we should be ready to become available for the service of God. The animals, including the fish, fowls and creeping things mentioned in this chapter, refer to persons with whom we may come into contact in our pilgrimage. They are often characterized by the very features which are found in these creatures. To eat of them would show a desire to mingle with them or to join them, although by virtue of their uncleanness they would only defile.

We can raise others to our level without sinking down to their position. How often do we find the principle adopted by many who would associate with the wrong company in order to influence them. How many of our young ones often take this dangerous step by forming such an unequal yoke and thus following a course which is contrary to the teaching of the Scriptures. A man will always be known by the company he keeps and will be influenced by those with whom he associates.

The Word says, "Sanctify yourselves, and ye shall be holy; for I am holy" (Lev. 11:44). This important instruction should transform our lives and compel us to examine our interpersonal relationships. Are our motives right or are we just interested in the worldly pursuits of our companions? We are not called to come out of the world but to remain undefiled while we are in it, and we have some responsibilities to those we meet day by day. No one was nearer to people then the Lord Jesus himself who remained spotless and undefiled while seeking and saving the lost.

It is possible for God to place us in a position where we have contact with persons who are unclean, yet we can serve them faithfully if we are truly influenced by divine grace. This is quite different from having friendships or courtships with unbelievers without being called of God for a definite purpose.

When we consider these first eight verses referring to the "beasts of the earth," we are told that the clean beasts have a cloven hoof and they also chew the cud.

The animals considered as prohibitive were the solipeds, or those with one hoof as the horse and the ass; while those which were regarded as edibly clean were the fissipeds, or those with the hoof divided into two parts, or cloven, such as the oxen, the deer, the sheep and the goat. We shall be considering these in a later chapter, but let us here confine ourselves to those mentioned in the verses before us.

When we think of the animals with the cloven hoofs, the question naturally arises as to why such creatures are clean. The answer is, to a great extent, wrapped up in the circulation of the blood and excretion of waste matter through perspiration.

If the feet are completely covered by a hoof, they will not perspire freely and therefore have no contact with the air. It would be tantamount to uncleanness, and a parallel might be found in a man wearing boots without ever taking them off. Such an animal with a covered hoof would be subject to disease that would escape the notice of the casual eye and this would increase the danger of eating flesh which could be unfit for human consumption. On the other hand, a cloven hoof will allow free perspiration and contact with the air; while any existing disease of the feet would be easily noticed before there is any danger of consuming unclean flesh.

God is naturally concerned that our bodies should be fit vessels. In partaking of food that is pure we are able to give Him of our best in service.

The second qualification for fitness is that all clean creatures must chew the cud. This means that any food eaten is chewed, swallowed, brought up and chewed over and over again. Providing these animals also have the cloven hoof, they are pronounced clean.

Those animals which chew the cud are referred to as the

ruminants, which suggests musing. They have four stomachs. The first is called paunch (*rumen*) and receives the food after it has been moderately chewed. The work is then taken over by the second which is called the honeycomb (*reticulum*). When the beast eats, it takes in as much as it is able, as fast as it can, and then lies down to ruminate. While ruminating, the two stomachs begin to dilate with the pressure of the food which has not been fully chewed and which swells with the heat of the body. The food then passes back into the mouth for a second chewing so that it is rendered softer before passing into the third stomach, called the manifold (*omasum*). From there it passes into the fourth stomach (*abomasum*) where it is softened and soaked until it becomes a white, milky fluid called chyle. From this it will not be difficult to see that chewing the cud indicates that, if the food is regurgitated over and over again, the result will be a good digestion and a healthy body. This will ensure that the animal will have clean flesh for man's consumption.

This may, of course, sound very technical and we may be excused for asking where such knowledge is leading us. However, it is obvious that, when God laid down these rigid rules, He also had some important lessons for us to learn and consider in our desires to maintain our standard of tidiness such as should form a part of our everyday life. Here we learn a manner of walking which should be consistent with our testimony. This is so that when we confess to the unsaved that we have surrendered ourselves to the Lord Jesus Christ, there will also be outward visible signs of that surrender.

Let us then remember that all clean beasts have a cloven hoof and also chew the cud. We shall see later that all these with a cloven hoof have a very careful manner of walk. This indicates a separate walk which should mark a holy people walking apart from the things of the world and its earthly principles. This separate walk by professing Christians can, however, be void and lifeless unless it is accompanied with an inward knowledge of the heart and mind of God. This is only possible if we are continually fed on the living Word of God so that it becomes part of our very lives. This feeding is typified in the animal which chews the cud or ruminates. To ruminate speaks of meditation; it means to ponder. Likewise, when we take in God's Word, we need to meditate upon it and chew it over and over again until the Word becomes an integral part of our spiritual constitution.

Jeremiah says, "Thy words were found, and I did eat them; and thy word was unto me the joy and rejoicing of mine heart: for I am called by thy name, O LORD God of hosts" (15:16).

We shall also find the idea of meditation recorded in Luke's Gospel when he tells us that, "Mary kept all these things, and pondered them in her heart" (2:19).

Unfortunately, it is all too easy for us to miss so much by not meditating on the things read. How many read their daily portions of God's Word without chewing the cud, meditating or pondering over the deeper spiritual lessons which we can learn as a result. A dear saint of God was asked how he was able to gain such an insight into the Word of God, how he managed to find such deep truths and hidden meanings in that he had received so little schooling. His reply was, "Well, I read a little and prayed a lot." Here indeed was a spiritual chewing of the cud which resulted in a healthy, vigorous, spiritual, born-again Christian walking carefully in accordance with God's Word and who was linking his separate walk with his prayer life. This careful walk must go hand-in-hand with a life of prayer and neither of these two important factors can be divorced from each other.

Sadly, there are those who attempt to separate these two important standards which are needed for a holy life that gives pleasure to the Lord. He has therefore shown us that some of these beasts of the earth, like the camel, chew the cud but do not have the cloven hoof. These are like some believers who know the truth, feed on the living Word and even meditate over it, but, nevertheless, they do not walk in the light of truth which they have received. Can it be possible that the Lord can find those who are content to fulfill only half of God's law in their hearts? It is so easy for really born-again Christians to be taken up with divine things, to be so occupied with doctrines of great truths, yet show nothing which reveals any evidence of feeding on the living Word. How many believers will gather regularly around the Word of God and even become spiritually fat on it, but do nothing more about it because they fail to find the time to put what they glean into actual practice? It is really incredible that it is possible to spend time studying yet to find no time to devote to the evangelization of lost souls. How many lost souls could be won for the Lord if we made our Christianity as practical as the amount of reading and meditating which is done around the Word.

Some believers are like the swine which has the cloven hoof but it chews not the cud. There are those who have the right kind of walk but who have no inward knowledge of the mind of God because they do not meditate on the Word—they do not "chew the cud." How often such will rush into the service of God without first meditating as to His will in the matter. How often we find young converts who should be feeding on the "milk of the word" (1 Pet. 2:2), being thrust into active service to preach to unbelievers before their time. How often such are at a loss for the right answer when asked tempting questions by opponents at street corners. Instead of being strengthened, they are weakened because those who have the responsibility for their pastoral care have not given them the essential opportunity to meditate upon the Word of God so that they can adjust their walk accordingly.

There are also those who are careful in their outward appearance yet fail to meditate. They are like the ones Jesus addressed himself to who were very meticulous about their outward appearance, yet had nothing in common with God. The Lord confronted these individuals very sharply when He said, "Woe unto you, scribes and Pharisees, hypocrites! for ye make clean the outside of the cup and of the platter, but within they are full of extortion and excess" (Matt. 23:25). "Woe unto you, scribes and Pharisees, hypocrites! for ye are like unto whited sepulchres, which indeed appear beautiful outward, but are within full of dead men's bones, and of all uncleanness" (Matt. 23:27).

May we learn how to feed on those things as shown in holy Scriptures, bearing in mind that God seeks a holy people who are also prepared to be "a peculiar people unto himself" (Deut. 14:2). Therefore, we need the double qualifications of the careful walk and inner meditation, as typified by those creatures with the cloven hoof and the chewing of the cud. In the same way as such beasts of the earth are pronounced as good, pure, wholesome food, we can also become pure and wholesome unto the Lord God.

Furthermore, we are not left alone to battle in our own strength, but, to our joy, God has made ample provision at Calvary. This, together with the power of the Holy Spirit, and the Word of God, joined with the word of our testimony, is sufficient to enable us to overcome. Thus equipped, we can be "more than conquerors through him that loved us" (Romans 8:37) and gave himself for us. It is He who has shown us the way, because He is the way, the truth and the life, and He has shown us how to walk prayerfully and carefully in His steps.

# 8

# Those in the Waters

Among the beasts described in the previous chapter we found that none qualified as clean if they had certain deficiencies. Some people are like the camel that chews the cud but has no cloven hoof, while others are like the swine that has the cloven hoof but does not chew the cud. Some Christians know the way but do not walk in it; others attempt to walk in the light without meditation which is so essential. We are to "walk in the light, as He is in the light" (1 John 1:7).

There are many things in the lives of believers which do not give the necessary indications that we belong to God, and that He has redeemed us through His Son. Many of our actions mar our personal testimony so that our manner of living, conduct and conversation fails to set an example which reveals our love for Him.

So many become smug and comfortable in their salvation without giving thought to the lost souls bound for a Christless eternity. How often the unsaved are turned away from the gospel through our behavior, so that we become unfruitful. These inconsistencies are found in all believers from time to time, and we can never claim perfection or infallibility, but we do have the assurance that "If we walk in the light, as he is in the light, we have fellowship one with another, and the blood of Jesus Christ his Son cleanseth us from all sin" (John 1:7).

We now find in our study of Leviticus 11: 9-12, that our attention is drawn to those creatures that are in the waters and described as abominable. It would seem also that, while we have had previous reference to the unclean, there is an obvious distinction between that which is unclean and that which is abominable.

In spite of our inconsistencies and shortcomings, we are assured of the cleansing power of the blood of Christ if we wish to avail ourselves of such cleansing. We also know that what God has cleansed is certainly clean. Nevertheless, we know there is a continual need for personal heart-searching and a willingness to allow Him to reveal to us those matters in which we fail and which result in much spiritual weakness and unfruitfulness. The saints of God should always be in a position to give a good reason for the hope that is in us (1 Pet. 3:15), and the beauty of Jesus should always be evident in our walk, behavior and conversation. If we fail in these respects it is because there is something unclean about us and we should seek to put matters right and claim forgiveness from the one who is "faithful and just to forgive" (1 John 1:9).

Having been given grace to accept our failures and having received the Lord's forgiveness, we then need to beware that we may forget the revelation and thus fail to act on it. This is an abomination in His sight.

An abomination is that which is hateful or detestable, and we find this word given to us in Genesis 46:31-34. Prior to Israel's entry into Egypt, a band of nomads, or the shepherd kings had made an invasion of Egypt and inflicted much cruelty upon the Egyptians. This was always remembered by the Egyptians, so that the name of nomad, or wandering shepherd, was one which they grew to hate. When Israel and his family arrived in Egypt, the land was probably ruled by a Pharaoh who was one of the shepherd kings and thus he was favorably disposed to Israel and his sons if they declared that they were shepherds.

Later, in Exodus, chapter 1, we read of a new king over Egypt who was not friendly toward Joseph. Apparently, the shepherd king was overthrown and from then on everything connected with shepherds or sheep was hated and detested.

Idolatry was looked upon as an abomination, and Jeremiah spoke very forcibly about the desolation which would come about in Judah through idolatry (chapter 44). Isaiah speaks of those who have chosen their own ways, and whose souls delight in their abominations (66:3). During the reign of King Josiah, all those things which were an abomination were broken down and cast out at that king's command.

These later incidents arose after the dietary laws were given, but the children of Israel would have realized from implication what the Lord meant when he described anything that was detestable or hateful as abominable. They could apply this to certain creatures and would know that such had to be cast out. Likewise, believers need to see that such abominable traits in our own lives should be cast out once they have been revealed to us. It is an abomination unto the Lord for us to actively continue in evil and we thus need to be definite in our refusal of all sin if we are to be a holy people of God.

We can now look at those creatures described as an abomination in Leviticus 11, verses 9-12. Here we read: "These shall ye eat of all that are in the waters: whatsoever hath fins and scales in the waters, in the seas, and in the rivers, them shall ye eat. And all that have not fins and scales in the seas, and in the rivers, of all that move in the waters, and of any living thing which is in the waters, they shall be an abomination unto you: They shall be even an abomination unto you; ye shall not

59

eat of their flesh, but ye shall have their carcases in abomination. Whatsoever hath no fins nor scales in the waters, that shall be an abomination unto you."

Water in Scripture imagery often signifies trouble. When we speak of anyone going through deep waters, we mean that they are experiencing much suffering. Waters also represent certain elements which every believer has to pass through in life, and these contain many temptations and evils as the natural waters contain many abominable creatures. Of these fish of the seas only those which have the double qualification of fins and scales are pronounced clean. The masses of fish are like great masses of humanity who combine together in great cities and have their trades or business combinations, giving no thought to the claims of a holy God.

Any fish breeder knows that fins allow the fish to steer a definite course without being at the mercy of the tides and currents. Such can be seen swimming in the pond or aquarium with its dorsal and pectoral fins well extended and, as it swims, it can move with a definite purpose. With its fins in full use, the fish will swim even more against the tides and currents, avoiding all infected parts of the water instead of drifting with any scum that might be washed down by the unclean water.

On the other hand, a sickly fish is soon discovered for its fins close in to the body and it just flows aimlessly with the currents and tides, not caring where it drifts. It will get caught up in every filth and infection, like a lost soul caught up in every wind of doctrine. Such souls merely drift with the tide and have no spiritual direction or firmness that is so essential to every believer. The same quality of decisiveness that is needed in a healthy fish is equally necessary for the Christian in order that he may resist and conquer the prevailing current of public opinion and lawlessness.

Lot is a good illustration of one without fins and who was not led by the Holy Spirit. We read that when there was strife in Genesis 13, he and Abraham agreed to go separate ways and Lot "lifted up his eyes," looked around at the fertile plains, and chose what seemed to him to be the best choice for he saw the plain as if it was the "garden of the LORD." It appeared to be all that could be desired; but then we see how confused he was in that he could liken the garden of the Lord to the land of Egypt. He was so mixed up that he was unable to discern the difference. How often the enemy of our souls will put something before us that looks like the path of faith so that we may think it is of the Lord. If we view everything with the eye of faith, however, and in the power and activity of the Holy Spirit, we will see things as the Lord himself sees them.

Lot was not properly guided. In fact, if we view his life up to this stage, we will see that he had traveled with his uncle during that unfortunate journey into Egypt and had become worldly minded. In all the circumstances he kept close to Abram but was just a "hanger-on" because he had no power to stand alone.

He thought of his own interests in a self-seeking attitude without any gratitude or respect for his uncle who had done so much for him. Perhaps Abram had often spoken to him about the precious promises of God, about the true manner of worship and the idolatry of the people from whence they had come. Lot's worldly mindedness was leading him to separate from his uncle and put the world first and foremost in his mind. He chose the way which only led him into great trouble; and, being tempted by the apparent fruitfulness of the land, he gave himself no time to pray or meditate as to the will of God. Then, forgetting his duty to Abram, he trusted his own eyes. How we need to ponder the path of our feet (Prov. 4:26) "and let all thy ways be established." How different was Lot than the godly man described in Psalm 143:8-10 who could say, "Cause me to

61

hear thy lovingkindness in the morning; for in thee do I trust: cause me to know the way wherein I should walk; for I lift up my soul unto thee. Deliver me, O LORD, from mine enemies: I flee unto thee to hide me. Teach me to do thy will; for thou art my God: thy spirit is good; lead me into the land of uprightness."

We find that, because Lot went the way of the world, seeking no guidance, he suffered greatly for he is seen drifting aimlessly through the currents and tides of the conditions in Sodom just as the finless fish. Think of his terrible end when, even though he urged his family to escape Sodom's judgment, his own family thought he was only joking. How terrible are the depths of degradation into which we may fall if we turn our eyes in the wrong direction and away from the Lord who is ready and willing to guide us through the storms of life. Lot was just a "hanger-on" and a drifter. He followed no definite course and was swept away by the conditions around him.

Lot, nevertheless, is described by Peter as "just Lot" (2 Pet. 2:7). Perhaps his righteousness stands out in contrast with Sodom's wickedness, for we see him being hospitable to strangers. He had a peculiar mixed character which allowed him to dishonor his own daughters; yet the accusations of the Sodomites that "This one fellow came in to sojourn, and he will needs be a judge" (Gen. 19:9), suggests that he had some sense of decency left in him. But he was so fainthearted, so irresolute, finless and without spiritual strength.

On the other hand, we may say that Lot had the second qualification needed in a clean fish, namely scales, to keep out infective influences. Scales act as a protection from the corrupt conditions in the waters. Any fish losing a scale is immediately in danger of infection. A fish breeder knows that the creature must be separated from the others and be placed in a solution of permanganate of potash in order to prevent disease. The fish will then have to be carefully tended and observed until a new scale is formed.

From a dietary point of view, it is thus obvious that a clean fish is well-protected from disease. Because of this, it may not be safe to eat other kinds.

The same Hebrew word *qasqeseth*, translated *scale*, is used in describing the impregnable coat of mail worn by Goliath. From this we can see that there is a lesson on complete separation from the world while living in it. How wonderful that the Lord could say of His followers, "They are not of the world, even as I am not of the world" (John 17:16), while Peter tells us of the "great and precious promises: that by these ye might be partakers of the divine nature, having escaped the corruption that is in the world through lust" (2 Pet. 1:4).

Neutrality in the presence of evil is worse than being in the evil itself and we should be able to form a right estimate of what is in the world. It is not just unclean but it is an abomination. As in the story of Lot, we can see how the great religious and secular combinations in the world would seek to crush our individuality and force us to fall in with their principles and methods. It is a Christ-rejecting world which men seek to build and it is a world which is marked for judgment.

The Lord has nothing in common with the world and yet He moved among people with a definite purpose of calling sinners to repentance and offering them eternal life. He could mix with sinners and outcasts and still remain spotless and defiled. Truly, He is typified by the fish with fins and scales, able to carry out the Father's will and remain unblemished in the world.

As true believers we need to have spiritual fins and scales, following in the steps of the Lord, keeping our eyes fixed on the prize which lies ahead and keeping ourselves unspotted. Anything that falls short of this standard is not fitting for a holy people called to be God's peculiar treasure.

# 9

# Birds of Prey

It is interesting to note that, in Leviticus 11:13-19 and the corresponding section of Deuteronomy 14, no clean birds are mentioned. Deuteronomy does actually speak of "all clean birds" and "all clean fowls" without specifying them. Birds are often used as a picture of the devil in the Bible (see Matthew 13:4 and 13:19). It appears that the purpose of this is to warn us against the fowls of the air which catch away the good seed and also influence with evil intent. It implies, therefore, that the Holy Spirit would cause us to reflect on these birds.

Not that it should be our purpose to be occupied with evil; but when we know something of the supernatural power of the enemy we know how to combat it and resist his fiery darts. There is an obvious danger, however, of too much concentration on satanic influences as such may indeed convince us of the devil's person; but if he can so lead us to think of him to the exclusion of God, he will be quite satisfied. In our consideration of this, may we keep the Lord before us as we look at these birds of prey in order to discover how they warn us against the cunning moves and devices of the evil one and learn how to meet him and raise the standard against him in the full power of the Holy Spirit.

Be sure of this, we shall all have to face up to satanic opposition during our pilgrimage in the Christian life, and if the Lord chooses to draw our attention to so many of these birds, it is obviously of tremendous importance to us.

Let us therefore study some of the characteristics of these birds and endeavor to see what lessons we may learn from them, and thus possess the correct discernment to recognize them at the appropriate time.

In verses 13-14 of Leviticus 11 our attention is drawn to the eagle, the ossifrage, the ospray, the kite and the vulture.

We have a reference to the eagle in Deuteronomy 32:11-12. It "stirreth up her nest, fluttereth over her young, spreadeth abroad her wings, taketh them, beareth them on her wings." The Hebrew word for wing (*kanaph*) means utmost part or extremity. It also signifies protection or defense when used in Psalm 17:8, "Hide me under the shadow of thy wings" (e.g. "Give me your protection"). Jesus uses this same thought when crying over Jerusalem, "O Jerusalem, Jerusalem, thou that killest the prophets, and stonest them which are sent unto thee, how often would I have gathered thy children together, even as a hen gathereth her chickens under her wings, and ye would not" (Matt. 23:37).

The eagle is often portrayed as a rather hideous bird, with its bald patches on the head and neck. Baldness in Old Testament times was indicative of leprosy which is typified as sin; while a woman with her head shaven (1 Cor. 11:5-6) was regarded as a harlot. Thus we find that, in spite of its apparent kindness and affection to its young, the eagle has many negative traits to be avoided. It makes its nest in the high places. "She dwelleth and abideth on the rock, upon the crag of the rock, and the strong place. From thence she seeketh the prey, and her eyes behold afar off" (Job 39:28-29). Even the young ones are bloodsuckers and the eagle is found among the dead.

Those who are in Christ Jesus, the Rock, need to be awake to the ways of the eagle, for she is also there among the strong in Christ, looking for those who are afar off, those who are weak in faith or those who have strayed from the fold.

The eagle, with amazing vision, is ever ready to swoop down on the young kid or lamb that has strayed from the place of safety and is caught in the thickets. It will pounce on such like a flash and devour them.

Even those who are not believers, are without Christ and dead in their sins, are subject to these attacks, for "wheresoever the carcase is, there will the eagles be gathered together" (Matt. 24:28). These eagles, in the spiritual realm, can also be similarly very gentle and kind in appearance and yet, when we study them, we find that they are destructive. Believers should also welcome constructive criticism, but the destructive critics are a constant danger to the young in Christ and the unconverted who may be really seeking but fall prey to many an eagle, ossifrage and ospray.

The vulture and the kite are filthy, rapacious fowls who flock to the battlefields and elsewhere in order to find dead bodies. Like the eagle, they have a keen sense of sight which enables them to spot their prey afar off. They also live and satiate themselves among the dead. Job tells us that "There is a path which no fowl knoweth, and which the vulture's eye hath not seen" (28:7). We need therefore to watch for these spiritual vultures and be ready for their attacks with the Word of God.

The raven in Leviticus 11:15 is a bird of beauty with its fine, black, glossy wings and offers a great attraction to the onlooker. Speaking of his beloved who is the chiefest among ten thousand, Solomon tells us, "His head is as the most fine gold, his locks are bushy, and black as a raven" (Song of Sol. 5:11).

The Hebrew word for raven is *Orb* which also means to wait.

It never rushes, but patiently waits for the appropriate moment when all is quiet and open for attack. It will dwell in the deserted and solitary places while waiting to attack the lone individual who has forsaken the true place of refuge; or the soul who, though seeking, may not know where to look. The spiritual raven looks for these souls and, true to its type, attacks the eyes. Truly, "The eye that mocketh at his father, and despiseth to obey his mother, the ravens of the valley shall pick it out, and the young eagles shall eat it" (Prov. 30:17). Young believers should, therefore, learn to take counsel from older brethren and sisters lest they fall as prey to the ravens and are blinded to the deeper spiritual things so that they are eventually consumed by the eagle.

It is a sad thing when a child of God loses his vision and when he begins to think that he can cope without the fellowship of other believers. Isaac is an example of this in Genesis 27. His loss of perception and spiritual intelligence deprived him of realizing that he was being deceived by Jacob and Rebekah, so that he could not even pronounce a true blessing. Was his lack of perception traceable to a desire to gratify his natural tastes? Is this the beginning of a fall? Here is one whose tastes had diverted him from the mind of God and who felt that the feebleness and despondency of old age had come upon him.

There is no need for us to be spiritually weak so that we fall prey to the ravens, for God makes full provision for our strength and we can draw upon infinite resources of power in Christ. May we learn how to be "strong in the Lord, and in the power of his might" (Eph. 6:10). Isaac's eyes were dim when he should have seen more clearly what was God's purpose. His eyes were dim when they should have been anointed with the eye salve of the Holy Ghost. The Lord himself says, "I counsel thee to buy of me gold tried in the fire, that thou mayest be rich; and white raiment, that thou mayest be clothed, and that the shame of thy nakedness do not appear; and anoint thine eyes with eyesalve, that thou mayest see" (Rev. 3:18). Self-will causes the attack of the spiritual raven and will result in spiritual blindness and improper discernment. We therefore need to have the eyes of our understanding enlightened "that ye may know what is the hope of his calling, and what the riches of the glory of his inheritance in the saints" (Eph. 1:18).

In Genesis 8 we find that Noah sent a raven out of the ark, and it becomes a picture of sin and the sinner. The raven went to and fro until the waters dried up and it did not return to the ark. True to its type, it pursued its restless course in spite of the turbulence of the waters which were not yet abated; like the unconverted and unsanctified. So the raven goes to and fro, and those blinded by the raven-spirit do likewise until the day when it is dried and judgment is past. Only through the death of Christ may we be transformed and brought safely into eternal life. How easy it is for sinners to feel quite at home in conditions outside the will of God, for the world is still a place of adventure and excitement. It offers many attractions for the unconverted and unsanctified, and it still remains a place where the unclean and unholy can be content.

How unlike the dove-spirit which finds no rest among the troubled waves of this evil world, who knows that it is on a pilgrimage and that it has a home in the world to come. Such can only rest in Christ while journeying the darkness and waste of the world. Those who know and love the Lord can never be content as a backslider; and such a soul will never experience the spiritual joys imparted to a holy people while he remains in worldly conditions. The only real assurance of blessing is found as we return to our own company where the Lord is owned. As in the case of the dove, the Lord himself, like Noah, stands ready to put out His hand and draw us back into the fold.

There are four different words which are translated *owl* and

69

it is therefore not easy to distinguish the exact meanings, but the reference here seems to apply to those birds who love the desolate and solitary places like the raven. They are the night owls which include the night hawk, the little owl, the great owl, the hawk and the pelican. The screech owl mentioned in Isaiah 34:14 is also translated as night monster, probably because it resembled the barn owl which is known to us as the screech owl or white owl. They haunt the deserted barns and decayed buildings. While seeking its prey by night the screech owl makes a doleful and frightening sound which becomes even more sinister in the dreadful stillness of the surroundings.

These birds of prey prefer the night because of its stillness, and because it gives them the chance to attack without being seen. They are like those who prefer the darkness to the light because their deeds are evil, and they remain out of sight during the day.

As children of the light we are called to walk in the light and we have God's promise that the blood of the Lord Jesus Christ cleanses us from all sin (1 John 1:7). Let us remember, however, that this cleansing is only conditional. It leaves no room for those doctrines which allow loose behavior on the grounds that the blood of Christ will cleanse. While we can rejoice in the knowledge of God's grace in redemption from all sin, let us remember that this is only as we seek to walk in the light as He is in the light. Self-examination is always vital and we have to ensure that we avoid all contact with the abominations of the night doctrines, for "if they escaped not who refused him that spake on earth, much more shall not we escape, if we turn away from him that speaketh from heaven" (Heb. 12:25). Greater is the condemnation of these who know the way and yet do not walk in it, preferring the darkness of their sins to the glorious light which is in Christ Jesus.

The stork is also an interesting bird, its name in the Hebrew, *chasidah*, means piety or mercy. This certainly matches with its character for it is a bird of much tenderness.

The stork is a very solemn-looking bird which stands for several hours in the same position, giving the appearance of being in deep meditation. This is rather remarkable when we consider the surroundings it chooses for such a display of piety, for it seeks its food in the watery places. This is typical of many professing believers who put on an attitude of piety in order that they may be admired of men. They will put themselves through many kinds of physical discomforts, believing that their religious exercises are proofs of their piety. Yet these darkened souls are in fact found in conditions and surroundings which are unclean and unsuitable for saints of God. These spiritual storks, although appearing very pious, are ready to strike at any creatures who dwell in such an atmosphere.

These pious-looking individuals can be very dangerous because they not only seek their food in the watery, marshy places, but they sometimes build their nests in the trees and other high places. "The trees of the LORD are full of sap; the cedars of Lebanon, which he hath planted; Where the birds make their nests: as for the stork, the fir trees are her house" (Ps. 104:16-17).

They also have an unmistakable instinct for they are even intelligent of the seasons, as says Jeremiah, "Yea, the stork in the heaven knoweth her appointed times . . . but my people know not the judgment of the LORD" (8:7). How true it is that the archenemy of our souls knows of the future judgment of God, while many believers know so little. We tend to forget that we need to work out our salvation with fear and trembling (Phil. 2:12), and learn how to come before His presence with reverence and godly fear (Heb. 12:28), for our God is a consuming fire (Deut. 4:24).

We need to watch and pray that we do not fall as victims to

these terrible menaces who fly in the high places, even among the saints of God. In their high flying, they can cause great trouble to the fellowship, causing us to be fearful in our witness instead of brave. These high fliers instill doubts in the minds of some while claiming to have a higher knowledge of spiritual things so that they are nothing less than soul-destroyers.

Although they may be beautiful in appearance, there is every evidence that these can be recognized by their destructive element. Those who are holding fast to the pure Word of God will soon discern that these birds represent open opposition to the fundamental truths and doctrines once delivered to the saints. The pernicious doctrines which they expound are often in bold contradiction to the holy Scriptures—they deny their inspiration, reject the Fatherhood of God and minimize the atoning value of the blood of Christ to such an extent that those who live in the gain and assurance of the rightly divided Word will know that these false doctrines are of the darkness and not of the light.

Many of these fine looking birds of prey are actually religious infidels, teachers of false doctrines, higher critics who claim to have made important discoveries about the Bible; but these will seek to destroy the power of the Holy Spirit and God's authority by their destructive criticisms. These infidels will attempt to devour the unwary by making their attacks at a time when both believers and unbelievers may be passing through dark times of sorrow or when they are experiencing tests of faith. In attacking our eyes they aim to blind our spiritual vision, rendering us so low that we will not rush to the Word of God for our solace and instruction. The saint without his only measuring rod is thus unable to meet the enemy's further attacks. He loses the assurance of sins forgiven and is no longer able to stand upon the promises of God.

If the child of God is holding fast to the apostles' doctrine, once delivered to the saints, he will be able to recognize those false teachings and will know how to deal with them. They are often so distinctly opposite to the truth that they are not always a great menace to the trusting one. But there are some religious teachings which seem to uphold the truth, and like the very beautiful birds of prey, make a good show and pass as very fine creatures to the unwary. They will not always appear in bold opposition to the Scriptures, but will claim that their theories clarify and give a better understanding of them. Many of these systems are supported by eminent scholars who will attempt to reason out the mind of God as if they themselves were God. Such are ever learning without ever coming to a knowledge of the truth, which is simplicity in itself to a true believer. However, these higher critics, who claim such accuracy to the Scriptures, seek to hide the fundamental beliefs and doctrines once delivered to the saints.

We can thus see that while these birds may appear to be fine and beautiful, they are destructive, they are soul destroyers, and the world is full of such who are turning the weak from the truth.

Let us also remember that much learning in God's Word does not make us mad. Paul faced this accusation in his day and he could say that this was not so, for it is needful that we should know the works of the enemy and be prepared to oppose such false doctrines which seek to devour the truth and destroy it. Even a good theological training can be used for God's glory if these studies are accompanied by urgent prayer.

To those who are giving proper place to the operations of the Holy Spirit in their lives, there is no need to make a hard and fast distinction between scholarship and devotion. It should be possible for a good theologian to be a devout and pious scholar. Unfortunately, it is all too easy for some to achieve a measure of devotion without scholarship; or, conversely, scholarship without devotion. The two need not be divorced and we should always study to show ourselves approved unto God (2 Tim. 2:15) and prepare ourselves for the work of the ministry and the knowledge of the Son of God. Living in the power of the Spirit will ensure that we do not become "covetous, boasters, proud, blasphemers, disobedient to parents, unthankful, unholy, without natural affection, truce-breakers, false accusers, incontinent, fierce, despisers of those that are good, traitors, heady, highminded, lovers of pleasures more than lovers of God; having a form of godliness, but denying the power therof: from such turn away" (2 Tim. 3:2-6).

Thank God, we are more than conquerors and know that the Lord is able to turn even the greatest of errors into the truth and that He will use birds of prey to fulfill His purposes when He so desires. He shows that He is "Lord over all," and "King of Kings." He will use the unclean raven to provide Elijah with his daily food (1 Kings 17). It may be queried as to why the Lord should choose an unclean bird for such a purpose, but we also should remember that the law did not prohibit the use of the camel or the horse (both unclean as food) when it was necessary to bear food from place to place. Instances too numerous could be quoted of personal experiences of the saints having their needs wonderfully met, and great blessings obtained through the most unexpected means, showing that even unbelievers can be used of God to bring blessing to believers. Even false literature, read by the strong in Christ and the spirit-filled believers, has been known to turn them more closely to the Scriptures for verification. Out of evil, God is victorious and He will bless His own regardless of any attempts to frustrate His purpose.

We should, however, beware lest we limit the Lord, for He is almighty and "all things work together for good to them that love God" (Rom. 8:28). Let us therefore examine ourselves so that we may be free from subtleties and errors which can lead us away from the truth which has set us free. We can thus enter into a closer walk with our holy God and become a partaker of the precious promises which await a holy and separated people who are His own peculiar treasure. May we always remember that there are very able and educated people represented in the birds of prey who would seek to undermine the faith, like Babylon who is said to have become "a cage of every unclean and hateful bird" (Rev. 18:2). This is indeed a very solemn warning to us, for right in the very midst of Christendom, with its profession of the name of Christ, pernicious and soul-destroying teachings are being propagated. These so often aim at convincing man that there is no need for a new birth, no need of a personal Savior, that all will be well if we merely do our best.

This kind of teaching is not only found in the world, but is engendered by leaders and dignitaries who are revered and respected in ecclesiastical circles. Let us not speak of such as "good men," for in man dwells no good thing (Rom. 7:18). They are sinners who need a Savior. They know the Christian vocabulary, and the Scriptures, but they are an abomination nonetheless.

We are exhorted to eat only those fowls which are clean; and although our attention is only drawn to those which are unclean, it is as though God is saying, "Go on with what is right, pure and holy and abstain from evil." When we see things that are not of God, it is well to avoid them and pursue that which is spiritual.

# 10

# Winged
# Crawling Things

"Yet these may ye eat of every flying creeping thing that goeth upon all four, which have legs above their feet, to leap withal" (Lev. 11:21).

We have seen in the previous chapter how fowls were associated with the works of the devil and are thus held in abomination. This is found in the lofty flights of a godless culture which springs from the evil one who is behind all sorts of proud materialism, the doctrine of evolution or a teaching that puts science before God. All this is an abomination to be loathed and avoided by the Christian.

There is also a class of "fowls that creep" and this completes the reference to the fowls of the air. These are not only associated with the devil, but they are also earthbound and therefore creep. However, there is a class which may be eaten although it can fly and creep. These are those which have legs above their feet with which to leap, while some merely grovel in the dirt and filth of the earth and are unable to use their legs to leap. The winged crawling things appear naturally unclean but the law pronounces them clean and fit for human consumption because of their ability to rise above the earthly conditions and temptations of the world because they have legs. When we are faced with similar problems during our pilgrimage we should be able to overcome them in the power of the Holy Spirit. We can, therefore, learn an important lesson from the particular characteristics of these creatures, because they are not earthbound but can leap up towards heaven.

There is a particular class of creatures which may be eaten although they fly and creep. In the same way there are certain secular, materialistic activities which belong to an evil world and are used by many for sinful purposes, yet the believer may use these things for God's service.

Music is an example of this. It is used in a godless way in certain quarters, even in devil worship. Yet how often it has enhanced Christian worship and been a means of drawing people to God through its sanctified use by faithful servants. Music can be mightily used of God for His glory or it can "fly and creep" and do much harm.

Printing is another instance of this for it also "flies and creeps" as it goes about its great business. It can serve the devil as it propagates false ideas, contempt for the truth and much filth. Yet, thank God, it is also as one that flies and can leap towards heaven in that it has been the means of making the Word of God available to the world. Christian publishers have used printing to publish literature and gospel tracts which have had the seal of God's approval, and have been used in the conversion of souls and other untold blessings. Truly, the Christian may fully use this printing for God's glory.

The locust, although nauseating in appearance, is a very persistent creature which does not easily give up and will fight to the end when attacked. A visitor to the Holy Land, in relating an attack of locusts upon a village, wrote that the inhabitants dug trenches and kindled fires, but eventually had to give up the battle against them. No matter how the people attacked the locusts, they came in great victorious hordes, typical of the power of God which no man can frustrate.

When the saints of God are filled with His power, no man is able to hinder the Lord's work, for He alone is mighty. Herod, in his raging, could not prevent God's purpose. Even the fierce opposition which the Lord Jesus encountered during His earthly ministry could not hinder Him as He set His face like a flint to go to Jerusalem and His death upon the cross. Truly, "the light shineth in darkness; and the darkness comprehended it not" (John 1:5)—i.e., the darkness could not put it out and that light has endured in spite of persecution. The suffering church can never be extinguished and will stand firm until He returns to take us to be with himself.

The Hebrew word for locust, *arbeh*, includes all kinds of this species of insect. About forty different types have been identified which go by the name of locust. Sometimes the word is associated with God's judgment. The suggestion is that natural phenomena, historical events, or human activity, which warn of impending judgment, can be used as food for a holy and waiting people.

The beetle has traits and habits which are similar to the locust. It has the Hebrew name *chargol* which is only used in this particular context. The beetle is felt to be of the locust family, being possibly the kind the Romans called *cossus*.

The grasshopper (Hebrew, *chagab*) is the smallest of the locust tribe and it is a very timid creature, expressive of humility. It is mentioned in Ecclesiastes 12:5, "And when they shall be afraid of that which is high, and fears shall be in the way, and the almond trees shall flourish, and the grasshopper shall be a burden, and desire shall fail." From this we know that grasshoppers are to be found in multitudes. They never forsake the gathering together and are very faithful to each other. They are a spiritual lesson to us, for as they are a burden to the outside world because of their faithfulness to each other, they show how we also can be a burden and a rebuke to the unbeliever, by our holy characteristics which are evidence of our deep love for the Lord. This love for the Lord is also shown in our love for each other, for herein we know that we love the Lord in that we love the brethren.

The Bible permits the eating of grasshoppers and they were widely eaten in the ancient Near East. The exact definition of the true edible variety has been obscure for a long time, but there is an old tradition which states that the edible variety has a distinguishing mark of the Hebrew letter *het* on its abdomen.

Another interesting characteristic of grasshoppers is that when they are cold they gather together, just as the children of God who need a renewal of warmth and vitality will gather together. When the grasshoppers have taken in the warmth of the sun they are revived by the life-giving rays, and are then strengthened to fly away and attend to their business. Likewise, we receive and enjoy the fellowship of the saints, are then encouraged, exhorted and strengthened to go into the world and proclaim the gospel to every creature.

We thus see that these creatures have legs above their feet with which to leap, and this speaks to us of spiritual energy of a Spirit-filled believer. This leaping comes to mind in the incident of the impotent man. Peter says, "Silver and gold have I none; but such as I have give I thee: In the name of Jesus Christ of Nazareth rise up and walk" (Acts 3:6). There is something very attractive in Peter and John. They not only speak of the Lord as being the one who is able to help, but they demonstrate it publicly. The beggar received new life, and could move in the power of the Holy Spirit so that he gained superiority over his condition and circumstances. Are we superior? Are we demonstrating what we are as believers?

The beggar had no power within himself, but it was given to

him. Peter could demonstrate it. We can likewise say to the fainthearted, "Strengthen ye the weak hands, and confirm the feeble knees. Say to them that are of a fearful heart, Be strong, fear not: behold, your God will come with vengeance, even with a recompence; he will come and save you" (Isa. 35:3-4).

If we are concerned with a soul, God will confirm His purpose with the same demonstration of power. Peter played his part. He took the man by his hand and lifted him up. Then God moved for we are told that "immediately his feet and ankle bones received strength" (Acts 3:7). That was God's part! The man could leap up and enter the temple praising God, and is immediately linked with Peter and John so that he is identified with them in testimony. Here is a perfect response to the testimony of God presented to man.

The spiritual energy of the early church is further demonstrated in Acts 9, for we see how its members were edified and increased in a spiritual way. Like the grasshopper, they gave warmth to each other and could leap up and praise God in a healthy and vigorous condition in the local meetings.

We can learn much from the winged crawling things and should take the humble position that is typified by their lowly movements. Like the grasshopper, we can leap above temptation through the power of the Holy Spirit. Hence, we see once again the two great necessities—walking humbly with God and tapping the power of God. These traits are typified by the creatures with the cloven hoofs who also chew the cud; the fish with fins and scales, and now the winged crawling things.

# 11

# Those Who Go on Their Paws

"And whatsoever goeth upon his paws, among all manner of beasts that go on all four, those are unclean unto you: whoso toucheth their carcase shall be unclean until the even. And he that beareth the carcase of them shall wash his clothes, and be unclean until the even: they are unclean unto you" (Lev. 11:27-28).

We now come to the chapter dealing with those beasts that go on all fours, but have not the two characteristics which are necessary qualifications to make a beast clean. These have no hoof at all but walk upon the pads of their feet. This may seem to be a contradiction to declare them as unclean as it has already been observed that a cloven hoof allowed ventilation and unrestricted circulation. One would therefore think that the animal without the hoof and the soft tread, having complete freedom of feet, would be more fit for consumption.

There are, however, three important factors to take into consideration regarding these soft-padded animals. First, many of them are beasts of prey who feed on human beings. When the law was given, many lions dwelt in the grasses on the banks of the river Jordan and, when the river rose, these beasts came inland rapidly. They would naturally have provided a ready source of food supply if they could be captured and slaughtered. Had the law allowed this, and such became food for man, this would have been a form of cannibalism which was strictly prohibited, for they would be eating flesh which had been sustained by human life.

The second reason for prohibition was that animals with soft pads are subject to diseases of the feet. It is obvious that, in the Christian walk, God intends that we should walk a careful middle course, for a foot which does not have a hoof can be just as unclean as if it had a hoof which is not cloven. This immediately suggests the narrow way in which we should steer the middle course lest we fall either way.

Thirdly, and this equally applied to the household pet, the skins of these animals do not all form free perspiration for they are not porous. They are, therefore, not healthy from a dietetic point of view and we can understand the prohibition. From a spiritual angle, we can see an even greater truth and learn important lessons as we seek the Lord's guidance in our study of these creatures.

These soft-padded animals would be of the wild and ferocious class, even through they have a majestic walk. The lion, for instance, is a typical example of such a beast and the Word of God abounds in figurative allusions to its habits and personal qualities. He is known by his ferocious roar and his soft tread. The sudden awareness of his presence is usually too late, for the lion suddenly leaps upon its prey without warning. This applies to all such beasts who walk upon their paws and have similar characteristics. It is sufficient to say that as they go on their paws they also have a soft tread. Their careful walk prevents others from hearing them. This can be seen in a miniature form if we observe even the ordinary household cat. The beast with a soft tread usually has a destructive purpose.

84

## Those Who Go on Their Paws

As we look around many fellowships of Christian assemblies, we find the false apostles and deceitful workers among them, pretending to be followers of the Lord while they are really satanic ministers appearing as angels of light. Unless we are awake and quick in spiritual discernment, we will not detect them among the saints and in the churches. Often it is too late by the time they are discovered and then we have to face the problem of getting rid of these evils. This becomes a dangerous task, for these evils are not easy to eradicate once they are too established in the routine of assembly life. To move them could also mean shaking the very foundations of a precious fellowship and losing half of the congregation who have fallen victims to these evils which have come in with a soft tread and whose aim is destruction, fear and strife among the brethren. Jude describes them as having "crept in unawares" (4). They have come in with a soft tread and a sly walk, unheard and with evil intent.

Since the first believers were established this has been happening. We see in John 21 how even the Lord's own words were misquoted. In verse 19 of that chapter, Jesus had been telling Peter that in his death he would glorify God, and He said to Peter, "Follow me." When Peter asked what was to become of that disciple, Jesus replied, "If I will that he tarry till I come, what is that to thee?" It did not take long for this statement to be corrupted by a misinterpretation that John would not see death. In fact, John himself found it necessary to clarify this. Unfortunately, the wrong idea was quickly established in the minds of the believers and it could have taken many years to eradicate this misunderstanding after it had become part of the teaching of the church. Something had crept in unawares to cause discord right at the very beginning.

Throughout the history of the church there have been those who have crept in unawares and it is possible to find such workers in our midst. They have entered unnoticed, unheard, but they are there just the same and are responsible for much error and misinterpretations of the Word of God.

Satan is always ready to oppose and spoil what God is doing, and this is apparent when we see his attacks upon the operations of the Holy Spirit in forming the body of Christ. The Acts of the Apostles shows us how the apostles were committed to stand against the devil in the Spirit's power, while the devil himself used violence, corruption and sedition. The Books of Timothy, Peter, Jude and the early part of the Revelation show us how God intervenes to make such opposition unsuccessful in the lives of these apostles.

During the Reformation, God intervened in great power to establish the truth of justification by faith and to deliver many from pernicious influences of the time. Unfortunately, the reformers of the day did not give the proper place to the Holy Spirit and consequently some of the false teachings were never fully overthrown. The state of modern Protestantism has for a long time been that which the Lord describes in His address to Sardis, "thou hast a name that thou livest, and art dead" (Rev. 3:1).

When God intervened by establishing the church and revealing the truth of her distinctiveness and heavenly character to her again, the devil renewed his opposition by sending counterfeits of God's power.

We know that God answers prayer because He is gracious. We also know that it is a matter of great delight to Him when we pray in accordance with the Word of God and are prepared to compare, test and judge our actions by the Word of God.

In our present day we are meeting with many subtle doctrines being expounded among the Lord's people. They would appear to be very accurate to Scripture and when we read the literature of these groups we could almost be tempted to agree. Alas, many give in to such temptations because they are either not spiritually alert to the works of the father of lies, or are not sufficiently grounded in the Word of God, which alone is our measuring rod and which contains all that is necessary to make us wise unto salvation. How essential it is for us to learn how to walk humbly with God and allow Him to teach us!

We could indeed point to instances of this in many Christian circles and wonder how many of these peculiar and false teachings came to be accepted, how such free license and lack of modesty and comeliness ever came about. Perhaps they were not noticed in the early days. It could be that we deceived ourselves into thinking that it was politic to give in to the whims and fancies of those elements who think that, by introducing certain innovations into our worship, other people will be attracted. It is, therefore, easy to find large gatherings attempting to stir up the Holy Spirit with the arm of flesh. This amounts to growth without spiritual intelligence and it has little in common with the mind of God.

How many companies are merely of the world and are encouraging our young people to form worldly associations? Such groups even claim dependence on the Holy Spirit's activity, giving God glory for their works of the flesh and yet denying Him His proper authority as head of His church. We now have a situation where our young people rule the elders and where the elders are afraid to act in case they lose their members. Women, under a cloak of so-called women's liberation, are usurping authority, denying the order of creation and the Lord's headship, and failing to accept their scriptural position when the church is gathered. Men, likewise, are failing to accept their full responsibility as good husbands and heads of the home. Thus the whole pattern of headship is distorted and reversed. Paul writes, "If any man think himself to be a prophet, or spiritual, let him acknowledge that the things that I write unto you are the commandments of the Lord" (1 Cor. 14:37).

True to type, this kind of insidious teaching and looseness has crept into the church very carefully, without fuss, without notice, with a soft tread, and a sly walk, while the church has slept. The devil has been very busy with his cunning devices, lulling many into a feeling of false security. There is little wonder why so many of our evangelical gatherings are not marked by God's blessing. Too often, meetings degenerate into just happy-go-lucky chorus singing led by worldly-minded groups offering inferior quality music, as if any poor or low standard is good enough for God.

A truly holy people will acknowledge that it is the narrow way in which we should walk. We may not like this way for it can be tough; but we can take up this challenge knowing that "we wrestle not against flesh and blood, but against principalities, against powers, against the rulers of the darkness of this world, against spiritual wickedness in high places" (Eph. 6:12).

It is possible to find a book written by a professing believer which has much to commend it, yet it can contain strange doctrine. This can creep in and become very dangerous leaven which ferments the whole lump. It may only be a small inconsistency in our interpretation of God's Word, but this can still throw the truth out of its proper perspective. Strange doctrines and practices can creep in. Thus we fail to experience the good hand of the Lord moving as was witnessed in the early days of the church. Such was witnessed also in times of revival when the saints pleaded with God to show them where they were wrong and unwilling to act on what God had shown them.

As we examine ourselves, we find that we are being attacked

by many of these "soft-padded animals." This is seen in so many false cults, such as spiritualism, Mormonism, and Russellism, which creep in and often have a ring of truth. Error can also be truth that is overemphasized, and we need to ensure that we take a firm stand, foursquare on the Word of God. We must be sure that we are not taking isolated texts and overshadowing them one with another, but taking and comparing them side by side. This is accepting the whole Word of God rather than a single text or part of one; for it is what the whole Word says, when rightly read and divided that matters. The Lord would not have a holy people contaminated by the abominations which creep into our worship through our lack of discernment and failure to realize the dangers of man's fleshly logic.

Let us therefore acknowledge the many weaknesses and evils which have crept into our church or assembly life. Let us recognize their origins and tell the devil he is a liar; that he was conquered at Calvary and has no right to any part of us. This will need much prayer from those of us who have the shepherd care over the flock, or those who have the oversight of the local company, for many will be offended by the truth. The Lord is able to deliver those who put their trust in Him, for He is Lord over all. Tell the devil to stand back in the name of the Lord Jesus Christ, and we shall claim, in greater measure, the blessings which our holy God desires to pour out upon a holy people who are chosen to be a peculiar treasure to himself.

# 12

# Creeping Things

"These also shall be unclean unto you among the creeping things that creep upon the earth; the weasel, and the mouse, and the tortoise after his kind, and the ferret, and the chameleon, and the lizard, and the snail, and the mole. These are unclean to you among all that creep . . ." (Lev. 11:29-31).

These verses from Leviticus 11 mention those creeping things which move slowly upon the earth and are pronounced as unclean. They have their habitat on the earth and have characteristics which are like those whom Paul describes as "enemies of the cross of Christ: Whose end is destruction, whose God is their belly, and whose glory is their shame, who mind earthly things" (Phil. 3:18-19).

We need to set our minds on things above and not on the things of earth, for those who are redeemed by the precious blood of Christ are subjects of a heavenly calling. If we fail to respond to this call, we become mere earth-dwellers with no assurance, no liberty, and no dignity. It was as earth-dwellers that men attempted to build the tower (Gen. 11). They cooperated and conspired together in order to deprive God of His glory, using brick for stone and slime for mortar, thus substituting what is artificial for what is natural.

From that day, man has had his own religion, his own civilizations, legal systems, social customs, and governments. All the various activities of man's life have been built upon his own earthly ideas and opinions and have little or no place for God's revelation. Man has built a Christ-rejecting, God-dishonoring world—a superficially happy and busy world, but in fact a miserable world. Man's earthly society is united by the bonds of false religion, common aggression and filthy mirth producing communications of unclean minds.

Young people should be shown how to seek the company of those who are spiritual, who call upon the Lord out of a pure heart, who can answer to the heavenly calling. There are always those who seek their own way, who do what is right in their own eyes rather than adhere to the things which have the marks of Christ. The most abject are those who walk in dignity but are merely content to live for self. Such are those that creep and are unclean in the sight of God.

Let us therefore examine the weasel, the mouse and the mole which do so much damage to the crops and young plant life. These animals are real pests to the farmer, for these little creatures work so quickly that they are seldom seen.

The weasel is a plucky little animal which lives on mice and is usually full of play and life. It is always tantalizing those who are going about their daily routine and is a reminder of those who find their way among the saints of God. These will mar the name of Christ by their careless witness in that they allow the wrong things to find a place in their lives. They are given to idle chatter and foolish jesting, forgetful that they have to give an account to God for every idle word that is uttered.

The mole does its work underground and disturbs the soil about the roots of the plants. The mouse, which is probably the field mouse, will nibble at the new and tender shoots, playing havoc with the fruit of the field.

The activity of moles and mice prevents growth in the same way as their spiritual counterparts who will check the growth of the saints and prevent the practical standard of personal holiness which the Lord desires to see in us. The damage done by these underground onslaughts often results in disaster because we are frequently unaware of the presence of these spiritual moles and field mice. Be sure of this, that as soon as we sow the good seed through the preaching of the Word of God, the moles and field mice will begin their work. The new convert is in great need of sound teaching based on biblical doctrine and will need feeding on "the sincere milk of the word" (1 Pet. 2:2). If this is not seen to by the elders and teachers, the moles and field mice will soon begin to hinder the growth of others. It will only require a few moles to disturb the soil so that it is no longer firm, becoming merely sinking sand. Then the field mice begin their nibbling at the very foundation of our new experience.

Our new converts will have to face the ridicule of sinners, dissension in the home, arguments with their colleagues at work, and even opposition from various religious and church groups who have a system of religion but are not walking in the ways of God. The new convert will soon discover how difficult it is to convince the religious man, after the flesh, that he is a sinner in need of a Savior.

Many perverse doctrines will be put forward in the hopes that the young convert will turn from the first principles of the faith that can only be grounded in Christ Jesus and supported by the whole Word of God. So much harm is done to the young and tender in the faith by these hidden sources of destruction. Yet this danger of attack is not confined just to the new convert; many causes of trouble and discord in the entire fellowship are due to these harmful works and interferences which are so difficult to trace. We often only see the corruptive influence of these workers of darkness after they have done their work and while they remain hidden underground. The real problem is how to put away the real motives of our actions which cause a lack of spiritual growth, vigor and grace.

May the saints of God become aware of the possibilities of such attacks and be ever examining the state of their spiritual growth. In the midst of our preaching and at a time when we are very active in our soul-winning campaigns, let us find time to ask ourselves whether we are growing in spiritual vigor and enjoying the great truths once delivered to the saints. Is the Lord finding pleasure in us? Does He come before all our activity? Are we so busy about the Lord's work that we are too busy to pray? If we cannot answer to these questions, and if we are not enjoying spiritual growth and vigor, let us look for these moles and field mice in our personal life and in our collective witness in the fellowship.

Our service to God should be in pleasing Him by being conformed to the pattern which He desires to see in us. When Moses was sent to Pharaoh, he was to say, "Let my people go, that they may serve me" (Exod. 8:1). Serving God, as Exodus requires, involves sacrifice. The Israelites were unable to offer such worthy service to God in Egypt. We, who are redeemed from the curse and the power of iniquity, are called to serve and we can only accomplish this by much prayer. The service of sin is cruel bondage, but the service of God is perfect freedom.

If we are not growing in a way which is pleasing to God; if God is finding no pleasure in us; if we are not bearing fruit; then let us look for the small things that are working underground. We may have to dig deep to find these hindrances, and when we have eradicated them we will find that we are set at liberty.

The tortoise is a slow-moving creature and a favorite household pet whose character is very much misunderstood. A healthy tortoise is free to move and wander wherever it pleases outside of captivity. When in captivity, it really suffers a gradual death, for once it is captured it hardly ever breeds. To capture our unclean thoughts will ensure that they are under subjection. We indeed have this power to overcome through the Holy Spirit. However, we will always need to keep our thoughts under proper subjection for, like the tortoise, the old man within us can live a long life. The things which we should not be doing we shall find ourselves doing, because, like Paul, we are wretched indeed (Rom. 7).

It has been said that the tortoise is one of the most difficult animals to drown. It will stand against the roughest of handling before it gives up, and although it may not breed in captivity, it will live in some way and endure the hardest of punishment before dying. Sin in our own lives may not grow if we keep it under subjection, but it will be hard to eradicate. Therefore, we must not fall into a cozy, snug frame of mind, for the enemy will continue his attack at a time when we are feeling comfortable. He that thinks he stands, let him take heed lest he fall (1 Cor. 10:12).

The tortoise will sleep when conditions are cold, but as soon as the temperature warms up it will begin to move slowly, and step by step, it will seek paths to explore. So when the saints are having a peaceful time without opposition, take care and get warmed up. At the same time, take heed for when there is life, vitality and warmth in the fellowship, the tortoise may well be found lurking. Capture it, keep it under subjection and do not be satisfied until the Lord has destroyed it completely so that the enemy will have no further claim on those who have been delivered.

The ferret has been likened to the hedgehog which is well known for its habits. It is a very unclean creature which digs underground after doing its damage, eating more than it needs.

One of its defenses is pretending that it is absent; but its camouflage is not as successful as it seems to believe, for it is quite easily seen.

If we remain alert, we will spot the kind of unclean character who will compromise the fellowship by worldliness. This compromise is often seen not only by the believers but, alas, by the world. How sad when the world sees in a believer that he is not upholding what is due to the Lord. Such behavior will do no good for anyone, believer or unbeliever, and only brings dishonor to the church as well as great sorrow to the fellowship. If we love the things of the world, we have not the love of God in our hearts (1 John 2:15).

We cannot, therefore, compromise in secret even though we may deceive ourselves into thinking that we can. "Be sure, your sin will find you out" (Num. 32:23), if you claim the things of the world while being in God's service. Achan attempted this when he committed his sin against God (Josh. 7). It was a sin which had a twofold enormity for he had taken that which was accursed as well as gold and silver which should have been devoted to God's treasury.

Israel, as a nation, had to learn how one man could bring such disrepute and grief. Consider Joshua's distress of soul when he cried, "O Lord, what shall I say, when Israel turneth their backs before their enemies!" (Josh. 7:8). He continued, "What wilt thou do unto thy great name?" (v. 9).

Nothing will ever safeguard us against defeat, or even overthrow, if we connive to do that which is contrary to God's will. Even prayer itself failed to compensate for neglect of discernment and proper action, for if we are not prepared to have God's revelation, we will not receive from Him. This sad setback came just at a time when Israel was entering its inheritance. They were one united people and, therefore, Achan's compromise affected the whole nation.

If we are a united fellowship, then we must take care and be warned against disaster through one who is going on in sin while enjoying the privileges of the company. As an example, Israel suffered disaster through the sin of one man—Achan—whose sin resulted in the disruption of spiritual blessing. Yet, Joshua is carefully guarding God's great name. This was pleasant to the Lord and Joshua was given grace to meet the emergency, discover the cause of the trouble and then execute judgment, sad and unrelenting though it was, for "all Israel had sinned."

One brother or sister compromising the fellowship involves the whole body and we need to walk humbly and carefully, refusing to have anything to do with the works of darkness.

The chameleon is a really attractive creature which does not appear very harmful. It feeds on insects and has a long tail which assists it when climbing or suspending itself. Its tongue is as long as its body and is covered with a sticky substance which adheres to its victim, rendering escape impossible. It can lie in wait, perfectly still for a long time, and with surprising ease and accuracy its tongue will dart out and catch small flying creatures with great speed. Even the clean creatures with legs to leap, such as the grasshopper and the locust, fall victims to the sticky tongue of the chameleon. How careful we need to be that the tongues of our enemies are not allowed to destroy our testimony; for the tongue is the most unruly of our members and can do great damage when used, particularly if we give cause for scandal.

The chameleon is not only known for its dangerous and sticky tongue, but by its ability to change its color according to its surroundings. This trait in a child of God is very much to be condemned, for the spiritual "chameleon" will also be known by his capacity to take on the color of his surroundings. The ease with which this change is so often carried out is somewhat distressing and bewildering to the Lord's people and to the world. This type of believer is quite at home with believer and unbeliever alike. He can change and vacillate to such an extent that when he is taking an active part in the assembly work and appears to be fully in the Lord's service, he is still enjoying the pleasures of the world. Such are at home wherever they find themselves. They are one thing in the assembly and another at home, in the office, the factory or the workshop.

The spiritual "chameleon" can maintain a witness in the assembly when given moral support, but he can also take an active part in other activities which are displeasing to God. This is unclean in God's sight and just will not do. What happens when the chameleon finds himself on a surface with mixed colors? What happens when this type of individual finds himself in the company of believers and unbelievers? Which side will he take? Who should he please? Let us not forget that our lives are an open book to Him with whom we have to do, and to the world.

Peter and John in Acts 3 obviously had something attractive to offer when Peter said, "Look on us." We might well say that they were young believers as they were not long in the faith. Nonetheless, they were certainly models for the testimony had started from them in a very new way. We might well ask what this man saw when he looked at Peter and John, or what did he expect to see? He had been asking for alms and they had nothing in the way of money to give, but they had spiritual riches and could demonstrate this fact in a very attractive way.

Can we say, "Look on us"? This should challenge the chameleon nature within us. May it touch us as we think of it. Are we at liberty to invite a stranger to a gospel meeting? If we are not being constant in our witness, or if our behavior with unbelievers is inconsistent, we shall only be in bondage.

If we tell a troubled soul to "look on us," or to "come and

see," we must also be prepared to have our lives examined. The visitor may know something of our past lives and that is unfortunate as there is nothing that we can do about that; but our present life is more important. Ananias had to learn the same lesson when told to go and find Saul of Tarsus. He remembered all that this man had done in the past and "how much evil he hath done to thy saints at Jerusalem" (Acts 9:13), but he had to be acquainted with up-to-date information, for Saul was now a changed man.

Truly, our present life and testimony must be able to meet with scrutiny when we offer an invitation to a gospel meeting. We will have to be prepared to answer to criticism by the way we conduct ourselves now. Our manner of walk, our testimony, our ways and our speech must be consistent both in and out of the church. The world knows what to expect of us. They may not agree with us but they will respect our consistency. The stranger will want to know whether we conform to the Word of God. Do we practice what we preach, or harder still, do we preach what we practice?

What then can the chameleon-spirit offer to seeking souls? Can we demonstrate to them the power of the Holy Spirit in love and grace? What do we hope to demonstrate to them when we say, "Come and see"? One thing is certain—we are inviting them to scrutinize, examine and criticize us. They will expect us to meet their standards without dropping our own, and we should attract them by our uncompromising behavior. They are expecting to see a separated people, a united people who are walking together in the living enjoyment of Christian and Holy Ghost experience, a people who are forthright in and out of the fellowship and who appreciate the presence and power of God in their lives.

At Philippi there was a place where the saints gathered for prayer, they shared each other's burdens, confided in each other, encouraged each other and their gathering was a powerhouse. The early Christians were directed by the Word of God and were more evidently concerned that constancy and attractiveness should characterize their assembly life. Paul could thus write to the church at Thessalonica, "Ye became followers of us." He could then continue "and of the Lord," and then, "Ye were ensamples to all that believe in Macedonia and Achaia . . . your faith to God-ward is spread abroad" (1 Thess. 1:6-8).

The chameleon-spirit will have to be accounted for if we persist with evil tongues and deeds, for these things are unclean to a holy and righteous God, and should not be found in a holy people.

Lizards, as a whole, would hardly seem to merit being in the category of the unclean, for they are not really very destructive. They are clean in their habits and make suitable pets because they emit no smells and carry no fleas as do other household pets. They are so fussy in their personal cleanliness that if a human being handles them they will merely take off the skin, which has been contaminated by human touch, and reveal itself in an entirely new one.

The lizard's Hebrew name, *letaah* from *lata*, means to adhere to earth or the ground. It can be seen running up walls and along ceilings of houses and its habits are interesting as they remind us of certain types of Christians.

There are those who are occupied with their own trials, and when they are among their own brethren, are ever ready to talk about their troubles. This type of "groaner lizard" usually enjoys his persecutions for they give him the opportunity to show his importance and to claim that he is suffering for righteousness' sake. Often the sufferings are due to his own lack of wisdom in dealing with the things of God.

On the other hand, lizards are exhibitionists. They are like the peacock which shows off before the other birds. The great red lizard displays itself so that it may be seen and heard in order to gain the admiration of man. It is like those who do their alms before men and whose reward is not found in heaven for they already have the approbation of men for their good works, and for their fine preaching (Matt. 6:1).

There are some believers who, like the climbing lizards, seek the important places in the assemblies. They are not prepared to be doorkeepers in the house of the Lord, or do common tasks, such as giving out hymnbooks and offering a friendly welcome to visitors. They are not content to stay in a humble position but desire only that they may reach the top. Such are those who revel in the respect of men and in their titles, and love to be called "rabbi, rabbi" or other terms signifying greatness. They desire the heights and demand the chief places at the feasts and marketplaces and are usually seen occupying the "important" places at the large conventions and campaigns.

The motives of their hearts can only be known by them and God. Those who are seeking honor would be only too ready to condemn important people having a box reserved for them at a theater, yet they are prepared to be spiritual climbers in the sight of God. The brother who refused to attend a campaign because he was not offered a seat on the platform is thankfully rare, but the lizard characteristic is possible in all of us. Such can be remedied by seeking God's help so that our weaknesses may be dealt with and that we may be strengthened to become like Him.

The snail is usually found in cellars and damp places, thriving in the very conditions where believers should not be found. Those whose deeds are evil prefer the darkness in preference to the true light of redemption. The snail will leave its mark in the form of a trail of thick, shining slime which in turn leads to its refuge in the damp darkness. It moves very slowly but is still not too easy to find for it usually knows when to move or stop.

The snail-spirit causes us to lose God's blessing because it places us in conditions not conducive to Christian growth. When this happens, we can discover the beginning of our weakness by following the slimy trail. Our search will take us through much dampness and darkness as we become troubled about our conditions; but God is ready to meet us when we are prepared to make a fresh start. Let us therefore keep our minds fixed on Him and claim the power to withstand any hindrances which come between Him and ourselves.

# 13

# Touch Not the Unclean Thing

Although Leviticus 11 is primarily concerned with eating, it also has some important things to say about touching. This chapter has reference to uncleanness which can be contracted from touching the carcases of unclean and clean animals.

In verses 24-28 we are told that whoever touches the carcase of an unclean animal shall be unclean until the even.

Uncleanness is infectious and can be communicated to one that is otherwise clean; but this condition need not be permanent. A Christian believer may either deliberately or inadvertently come into contact with things which are spiritually unclean. He may touch the unclean thing in a way in which God forbids and thus spoil his witness and corrupt his teaching to such an extent that he will never be free of the accusing finger. The church suffers much of its weakness today because of its contact and cooperation with the unclean. Lack of separation from sin and lack of godly witness marks us in these strange times.

The carcase would be carried, probably over the shoulder, so that it would touch the clothes; but whichever way it is carried, it renders the person unclean. Likewise, we need to watch because some may claim a good motive for touching the unclean.

It is very easy to come into contact with much of the world's uncleanness and verses 39-40 give us the case of a clean animal which dies. A sheep or an ox can lead some astray and a man of God is capable of neglecting his private reading and prayer life so that he may preach a dead word, yet his state may not be discerned by his hearers.

Such uncleanness is inconsistent with holiness yet it is possible for us to be very careless about these things. Some may even attend a meeting held by false teachers in the hope of learning something for edification, or perhaps for curiosity; but this can only serve to destroy the consistency of our witness.

Yet there is a very moving touch of grace here for we have the assurance that we can be clean in heart and conscience. Such will be "unclean to the even," means "can be cleaned by the evening." This tells us that it is possible to be washed clean; that the cleansing water is always available, and we have only to bathe in it the same day. This means that we need not ever carry our anger to the following day—"Let not the sun go down upon your wrath" (Eph. 4:26). Our lives are made up of individual days and the Lord would have us to settle every question of defilement and anger before the evening, instead of allowing things to fester for days and weeks, or even years.

How many assemblies have been stifled because a brother or sister is harboring some petty grievance which has become a festering sore, when it could have been settled by the evening. If we can take a daily review of our spiritual state and search our hearts for that which is unclean—i.e., any bitterness or wrath—we can settle our account by the evening.

A brother has a grudge—settle it by the evening and then you can lay your head on your pillow with a good conscience before God. Any such uncleanness will abide and leave its mark if it is not dealt with. We need the exercise of a loving heart and spiritual watchfulness so that we may have the sweetness of the Lord Jesus.

God's provision is very sweet for "a fountain or pit, wherein there is plenty of water, shall be clean" (Lev. 11:36). Pit means "cistern" and fountain speaks of "energy." So we have the power of the Holy Spirit, the fountain of living water and the Word of God. Neither the Word nor the Spirit can ever be corrupted, and if we hold fast to both we will not need to fear. If we want spiritual life and energy, we have a supply source. If we want to be immune from defilement, the secret is found in the presence and living activities of the Spirit of God.

If we have stumbled, there is still a way by God's grace, for under the gospel, the blood of Christ is still available. Lay everything bare before God, claim the cleansing power and He will say, "Behold an Israelite indeed, in whom is no guile" (John 1:47). Plunge into that fountain that is open for sin and uncleanness, for this is the only way to wash spiritual robes and make them white in the blood of the Lamb (Rev. 7:14).

> There is a fountain filled with blood
> Drawn from Emmanuel's veins
> And sinners plunged beneath that flood
> Lose all their guilty stains.

> (William Cowper)

God, through Christ, has a unique relationship with His people. This is all bound up in His plan of redemption. He has redeemed us from sin and death and He became our God and Father. He saves us because He desires to dwell in our hearts so that we may glorify Him and enjoy Him for all eternity.

The Lord calls us to be holy, separate and different, whatever the cost, and this leads to fellowship with God, and His joy is our strength (Neh. 8:10).

105

# 14

# Spiritual Food

In the previous chapters we have been considering ways and means of achieving the standard of holiness as required by the Lord God. From Leviticus 11 we found that God had not only set the standard, but that we are shown that in keeping certain principles and remembering various prohibitions, we can reach the required standards if we are prepared to set out to obey them with God's help. He has thus given us a textbook which, if followed closely, must result in the standards required of a holy people. These rules reveal that certain creatures, which are pronounced as unclean, typify different characteristics which are either unclean or abominable in the sight of God. Then, having learned how to separate ourselves from such things which do not satisfy the standards set by a holy God, and having reached this desired state by our separation from the world's principles, we come to Deuteronomy 14.

Here we find that, after we determine to please the Lord by sanctifying ourselves for His service, we become accounted worthy to be called the children of God. In verse 1 we read, "Ye are the children of the LORD your God," and we have entered into a family relationship with the Lord God and should be feeding only on those things which are characteristic of the Lord Jesus.

This personal relationship involves two important rules. The first is, "Ye shall not cut yourselves, nor make any baldness between your eyes for the dead" (Deut. 14:1). As children of God, who are created in His own image, any idolatrous mark would disfigure us and mar our testimony, for we are supposed to be a holy people, chosen to be a peculiar people unto himself. Any careless action or unsanctified move on our part will bring great dishonor on the Lord's name and on His people who seek to walk in the way. "If any man defile the temple of God, him shall God destroy; for the temple of God is holy, which temple ye are" (1 Cor. 3:17).

How solemn is the fact that a divine person, the Holy Ghost, can dwell where Christians are gathered together. This would not have been so without the work of Christ who died, rose again and ascended to send the Comforter to abide with us. This is God's testimony to the truth of that sacrifice at Calvary, and the Holy Spirit will dwell where that blood shedding is confessed. Thus God has His temple on earth which is not a structure of costly stones, nor of gold and silver, but the assembly of born-again believers who become living stones, builded and united together.

Some build well and wisely confess His name, building on the only one true foundation. But the enemy is always at work and will attempt to use men that bear the Lord's name to corrupt or destroy the spiritual temple. God resents that kind of evil which defiles the temple where His Spirit dwells, and He will surely destroy Satan's ministers who appear under disguise and pollute the streams of life and dishonor the temple where He dwells.

The second great rule is, "Thou shall not eat any abominable thing" (Deut. 14:3). We must now bear the mark of Christ in order that we may bring delight to God, and we are reminded that we must avoid anything that is abominable. It is as if God is saying, "Anything which displeases me is abominable," for we now know the way, and should be walking in it.

As we avoid those things which are an abomination, we must of necessity feed on those things which are characteristic of the Lord Jesus. In order to do this we need to walk in His steps. As He pleased the Father and answered to His pleasure, so we are called upon to do likewise by living on His characteristics and avoiding the abominable. These things have already been typified by those associations or influences which mar our testimony, the things which we allow to become part of our lives, the kind of company we keep and the books we read. The emphasis of this chapter is on the things which we are commanded to eat if we are to maintain our testimony and bring honor to the Lord, rather than the things which we should not eat, for we have already considered these.

Our associations should bear the marks of Christ, and as such they are evidence of our sonship. The company we keep and the books we read must have something of the Christ-like spirit; and that which is not of His character is totally unsuitable for holy children of a holy God.

Let us then look at those features which are so needful and which are seen in the clean creatures which we are commanded to eat while enjoying our family relationship with God.

Only those beasts which chew the cud and have the cloven hoof, typifying the inward rumination of God's Word accompanied by the careful walk, are clean. It is required, and is indeed demanded, that the saints must have both characteristics for one cannot be divorced form the other. Those who only meditate on the way but fail to walk in it are under the same condemnation as those who seem to walk in the way but do not meditate about it. Neither are of any practical value to the testimony of the Lord and are an abomination to Him.

Deuteronomy 14:4 and 5 now draw attention to those clean beasts which should be eaten. "These are the beasts which ye shall eat: the ox, the sheep, and the goat, the hart, and the roebuck, and the fallow deer, and the wild goat, and the pygarg, and the wild ox, and the chamois."

The ox is a well-known domestic animal which is strong and patient in labor, and is a great help to the farmer, for it is used for plowing and drawing. It is known for its strength in such labor and it is referred to in the Scriptures—"That our oxen may be strong to labour; that there be no breaking in, nor going out" (Psa. 144:14). "Much increase is by the strength of the ox" (Prov. 14:4)

Likewise it is written of the Lord Jesus, "Wherefore when he cometh into the world, he saith, Sacrifice and offering thou wouldest not, but a body hast thou prepared me: In burnt offerings and sacrifices for sin thou hast had no pleasure. Then said I, Lo, I come (in the volume of the book it is written of me,) to do thy will, O God" (Heb. 10:5-7). He came with all the capability of the ox to do all that was according to God's pleasure and He displayed the necessary strength to carry out the Father's will in every detail. This He accomplished with patience and with persistent energy and He could say, "He that sent me is with me: the Father hath not left me alone; for I do always those things that please him" (John 8:29).

It is said that the steady pull and drawing power of the ox is beyond comparison with any other animal, for it has no sudden fits and starts, no rushing or halting, but an even, onward, persevering movement which is typical of the life and service of the Lord Jesus. It is no small wonder that Mark records no less than forty times that Jesus went either "straightway" or "immediately" when called upon. We read how He passed from one service to another without any fuss or commotion. He was never in a hurry, never halting, but always ready to meet some need and then pass on without delay to His next task. He always put the service of God first while seeking to please the Father in all things. This example should shame us. As children of God, we should be feeding on the Lord Jesus as typified by the ox, so that we should be known by our spiritual strength and persistent toil in God's service. These should be the marks of our sonship, and evidence that we belong to a living God.

The wild ox mentioned in Deuteronomy 14:5 may be included at this stage. Although the wild ox is a clean creature, it has to be set to work by its master, just as we need applied tasks as we enter into the service of God. We are no longer free to please ourselves and run wild for we have been bought with a price—God's only beloved Son—and we have to learn how to bear the yoke of service and how we may thus please God.

Yokes were made with great care in the East so that they would be light and easy for the oxen to bear. The Lord, himself a carpenter, would know how to make a yoke and He tells us that His yoke is easy and His burden is light (Matt. 11:30). There are times, however, when, like a wild ox, we need rest from our labor. At such times we should make our way to the mountaintops where we can breathe in the pure air and prayerfully feed on the Word of God until we are called upon to undertake some new task in our ministry. The wild ox is also found on the mountaintops, away from the ordinary things of life, and its strength can most likely be attributed to this, so the traits and habits of the wild ox can also have a place in the Christian life. If we are prepared to feed on the Lord Jesus as so typified, we also will have a well-balanced testimony. We shall be conscious that our strength comes only from the Lord himself, and we shall be able to use this strength for His glory.

The sheep comes next in the list from Deuteronomy 14. This

111

animal has always been held in high esteem. The children of Israel kept many sheep and they often judged a man's wealth by the number of sheep he possessed. This naturally meant that care of sheep was regarded as one of the most respectable of occupations, as in the case of Abel (Gen. 4:2) and Moses (Exod. 3:1).

Abel was a keeper of sheep and God had respect for his offering which was "by faith" (Heb. 11:4). Doubtless, Abel believed in God's promise of a coming Messiah (Gen. 3:15). He saw this promise afar off, embraced it, was justified by faith and became the first "trophy of grace" gathered in from a lost and fallen race. He was thus accepted by God. He was a keeper of sheep but Cain was a tiller of the ground. The practice of agriculture and domesticating animals as seen here proves the error of the theory, held by modern anthropologists, that long ages of prehistory elapsed during which time man lived by hunting and fishing.

Moses kept the flock and must have found great satisfaction in the fact that he had made such a choice by denouncing the pleasures of Egypt. Those forty years as a keeper of sheep provided him with the essential training for leadership of the Lord's flock.

David also was a keeper of sheep (Sam. 16:11), but while sheep-keeping was regarded as an honorable occupation among the people of God, it was regarded as an abomination among the Egyptians. This is probably due to the fact that the early invaders were the shepherd kings. Our Good Shepherd, the Lord Jesus, will also be spurned until that day when every knee will bow at the sound of His name.

Sheep and goats mingle together while they feed, and this gives some meaning to the Lord's words in Matt. 25:32-33 that He will separate the sheep from the goats.

The chief characteristics of the sheep are timidity and

docility. When they go astray or run into danger, they are helpless until the shepherd finds them and is able to rescue them. The sheep knows its shepherd and will automatically listen for the sound of his voice when in trouble or distress. We could profit by emulating and developing the instincts of the sheep by keeping close to our Good Shepherd, so that we may also hear His voice and turn to Him who is our only refuge.

The sheep is not known by its strength, like the ox is, or by the steady and dignified walk of the goat, which will be our consideration later on, but by its uncomplaining submission and humility. This is typified in Isaiah 53, "He was oppressed, and he was afflicted, yet he opened not his mouth: he is brought as a lamb to the slaughter, and as a sheep before her shearers is dumb, so he openeth not his mouth" (v. 7). The Lord Jesus also left us a pattern of behavior to follow by showing the relationship of the shepherd and the sheep. We can also be imitators of Him. "For even hereunto were ye called: because Christ also suffered for us, leaving us an example, that ye should follow his steps" (1 Pet. 2:21).

In Luke 24, He is seen as caring for two men who were forlorn and disappointed. Here He is as the Good Shepherd.

We need to come in the consciousness of His authority in John 8, but also we need to see His mission of love for He was the Word made flesh, and to that end He went into death.

In John 10, however, we see that there is only one Shepherd who lays down His life for the sheep. He calls the sheep His own.

The blind man in John 9 received his sight and could now feel at home among the flock, for an entirely new world was open to him when previously all other doors were shut.

The features of Christ should always mark the company, whether they are viewed as sheep, children, or friends. These features maintain the testimony of our Lord.

The Lord's people are united, not in artificialities of formalism or orthodoxy, but in the vitality of His divine nature. In the same way that the sheep maintain a closeness under the shepherd, the Christian maintains perfect affinity with others who love Him.

May our characteristics be typical of the sheep who knows the sounds of the shepherd, so that we may be ready to be corrected by Him when we slip or stumble by the way, and when we leave the fold. As we call upon Him who is the only true Shepherd, He will carry us back to green pastures and still waters where we can feed on the pure Word of God. We should be feeding on His bountiful supply as seen in the way the sheep receives the right kind of sustenance when in the proper place. The sheep, as seen with its humility and acknowledgment of its helpless state, is a constant reminder to us that we can do nothing unless the Lord is with us to guide and strengthen us by the way. Unless the Lord builds we labor in vain (Ps. 127:1); but if we feed on the Shepherd as shown here, we shall walk as He walked, with humility and complete submission to the will of God.

Goats are mentioned among the chief possessions of the wealthy in early ages. They resemble sheep in appearance and structure, but are covered with hair instead of wool. They feed on bark and tender twigs and are much bolder than the sheep.

They are mentioned in Proverbs 30 as being among those animals which are comely in going, or stately in step. This is typical of the kind of walk required of children of God. Regardless of His circumstances and the varied conditions in which He found himself, the Lord was always stately and comely. He was found among publicans and sinners, among the unbelievers, the weak and the strong, amidst many misunderstandings, even from his own disciples; yet He moved with the dignity and comeliness that we see typified in the goat.

It has been said that respectability is the curse of mankind. This is possibly true unless it is motivated by a desire to serve God. Anything that has the wrong motive and directs us away from the simplicity which is in Christ, even in the guise of some form of respectability, can be a curse. Yet we would maintain that the Lord expects us to walk in dignity as children of God and that we should be respectable in our Christian life. We need to be clean and decent in our manner of dress and behavior, for He has not called us to be paupers and beggars.

Likewise, our gatherings should be decent and orderly so that visitors may experience something of the Lord's grace revealed in our worship, our evangelism and in other missionary campaigns. Think of the dishonor that can be brought upon the Lord's name by a disorderly meeting when so much is disregarded in the name of freedom. Such freedom is often misunderstood for license to do just as one likes without considering the mind of God and without stopping to think that we may be grieving the Holy Spirit. The gospel being preached by someone who does not possess proper dignity is of no credit either to our holy God or to our personal testimony. If the gospel is preached in such a disorderly manner as to grieve us, how much more will it grieve the Holy Spirit? We are called to holiness, and therefore should be walking with the same dignity and comeliness as is proper to such a high calling.

This is the way the Lord himself walked among the people; never halting, never perturbed, never uncertain as to what step to take in any circumstances. Even in the most uncongenial circumstances, He was comely. Even while He was in the presence of the devil himself, or among unbelievers, the Pharisees, the Sadducees, the chief priests, and Herod; while He was in the judgment hall; and even when He was on the cross, He carried himself with dignity, stateliness and comeliness in all His movements. Truly, He was submissive, humble and obedient, even to the death of the cross (Phil 2:8); and He never gave cause for rebuke. Only His greatness could make Him humble, for only the truly great can be truly humble. We can learn much from His dignity which we see typified in the goat, and can thus move in the same way as we walk in His steps.

The wild goat, now called the ibex or mountain goat, is confined to the high places, and it is often found on the most inaccessible summits of mountains. God delights to find the saints in high places also. Like the mountain goat which can elude its hunters by leaping as far as twenty feet and will hide in the rocks where it cannot be found, the saint who lives in the "heavenly places in Christ Jesus" will be able to escape from the enemy.

As we seek the mountaintops of our spiritual awareness and live in the full gain of that experience, we will obviously be exposed to all invading influences which will attempt to frustrate us and prevent us from the enjoyment of what God has done through Christ Jesus. When this happens there is a refuge and we can leap, with the same agility as the wild goat, to our Rock and Sustainer. Here is the place of safety; here is where we are able once again to be strengthened and encouraged to rise up in the full liberty of the Holy Spirit to face the evil one when he comes in like a flood.

It was the goat that was used as the scapegoat on the Day of Atonement, when laden with the sins of man he would be driven into the wilderness (Lev. 16). The goat would then find the heights and rise to the summit in the same way as our sins were laid upon our Savior who is now risen to make intercession for us. How truly we should be able to feed on such a truth and thus enter into the joy of this unique relationship with the one who became our Savior, who became sin for us, but is now alive for ever more.

The hart, the roebuck and the fallow deer all have very similar characteristics and we can therefore consider them together.

The hart, particularly, has some interesting features which should also be seen in the children of God; for it is a simple example of giving expression to an inward desire after God. The psalmist took hold of this thought when he used the hart to explain his own spiritual yearnings. He could cry, "As the hart panteth after the water brooks, so panteth my soul after thee, O God" (Psalm 42:1).

Throughout the whole Word of God we find evidence of the saints whose one desire was to please God. Many of them really panted after the water brooks, but the Lord Jesus himself is the one perfect example of such intensity. He sought to maintain what was due to God. He was engaged in the service and interests of His Father and was prepared to drink the bitter cup. Jesus desired to satisfy the heart of the blessed God to draw all men to himself through that death on the cross. Surely, He was panting after the things of God in a very real and practical way. Even in the temple as a boy we find Him engaged about His Father's business (Luke 2).

Later, in His desire to maintain the purity and cleanliness of God's house, we see Him overturning the tables in the temple; i.e., panting after the things of God. In all His movements and throughout His public ministry, He was ever fervently panting after the things of God. So He was willing to die—the just for the unjust.

As children of God, we also should be engaged in our heavenly Father's business. We should be ever ready to claim the cleansing value of the blood of Christ so that we are delivered from those things which bring disrepute to His holy name. Our desire should be after the things of God and we should thus be panting after divine matters as we feed on Him, as typified by the hart. If we can dedicate ourselves to Him and His righteousness with the same intense desire with which the hart pants after the water brook, we shall be ready to do those things which please Him.

In the roebuck and the fallow deer we have a suggestion of what is beautiful or glorious. The Hebrew word for roebuck is *tsebi* which means beauty, glorious and pleasant. What a lovely picture this is of the Lord himself who was fairer than the sons of men, full of grace and truth. What beauty and glory we see in Him as we liken Him to the roebuck which is so active. Like the ox and the goat, the roebuck lives in the high places. It is a loving, amiable and gentle creature. Unlike many of us, it is not easily upset or offended, and it takes great care of its young. Any new convert finding his way into a company of the Lord's people which possesses the qualities of the roebuck, would be fortunate indeed. He would be ensured of a warm welcome, the necessary pastoral care by the elders, and he would be carefully nurtured in the faith and be fed on the pure milk of the Word of God.

The pygarg and the chamois possess the same kind of characteristics as the hart family; nevertheless, the Holy Spirit of God must have found these particular features of great importance to duplicate them in the passages before us. Repetition in the Bible should always cause us to think because God would waste no words.

Much prayer and much grace will be needed if we are to be found walking in the light of what we have seen represented by the clean beasts. As we seek more and more of the Lord, we will become more conscious of the fact that we are bound to maintain the holiness of children of God as exemplified by the careful walk and inward rumination that is revealed by these clean creatures.

## Spiritual Food

What we appear to be externally may be very different from what we really are inwardly. Because we know that the Lord can see right into our hearts and minds, our outward testimony to unbelievers can only bring disgrace to God if it does not match with the things we profess. If we can feed on Christ, as typified by these clean creatures, we will always have Him very much before us. Therefore, we will desire to retire more and more from the world because we know that if we love the world it is because we have not the love of God in our hearts. Here is the evidence that we love Him—that we love not the world and are prepared to be lost to it until we are truly lost in Him. We find rest, hope, comfort and blessing near to His blessed heart and there we shall desire to do only those things which please Him. With the Christ-like features that are seen in these creatures, we can see something of the regard which God has for tender feelings.

In Deuteronomy 14:21 there is an injunction, "Thou shalt not seethe a kid in his mother's milk." This prohibition was undoubtedly given because of the obvious dangers of mixing meat and milk purely from a digestive point of view, as we saw in chapter 3. Modern medicine has confirmed the fact that certain mixtures of this kind create their own bacteria, even though they may be popular dishes. Such can be very dangerous if not treated with great care. There is also a great risk in preparing dishes containing blood. Creamed chicken generates ptomaine, and we still have much to learn as to the dangers of saturated fat.

It is also important to note that the instruction against mixing meat and milk is repeated three times in the law. Maimonides, who was a doctor, confirmed the health hazard, but suggests that the threefold prohibition was made in order to emphasize that God desired that His people should not emulate the common rite of idolaters. Nevertheless, we can still claim the importance of these repeated warnings and it is as if the Holy Spirit is alerting us to take heed when God speaks.

Let us not regard this law as just a harsh prohibition, for it is indeed an example of tenderness which should mark the people of God.

The natural mind may ask, "What does it matter?" Truly, it makes no difference to either mother or dead kid, but is it not pleasing to God for us to regard what is of himself in nature? The more we consider this relationship between the mother and the kid, the more deeply we can enter the feelings of others. We become more careful not to offend others by our thoughtless actions and compromising. It helps us to enter into their sufferings as our blessed Lord did when He intensely grieved after seeing the multitudes as sheep without a shepherd. He entered into our afflictions and took upon himself the burden of our sins. Now He has us all in mind in great tenderness and sympathy.

Our feelings, as children of God, will help us to refuse those things which will hinder others in fellowship. When we find ourselves in places where we should not be seen, we are taking our brethren with us. When we act as an individual, we act as part of the fellowship. If we sin, then the fellowship has sinned.

The relationship which exists between a mother goat and her kid is one of tenderness and understanding. This speaks to us of our relationship with our Father and His beloved children.

# 15

# Priestly Features

"And they shall give unto the priest the shoulder, and the two cheeks, and the maw" (Deut. 18:3).

When we study the Old Testament Scriptures, we cannot help being conscious of how they abound with references to various kinds of food. These references have a number of connections and circumstances so that there is ample provision to meet every possible contingency.

There is a reference to special portions which were to be provided for the priests, and it would profit us to take a brief look at these in order to see how it affects our own personal testimony, for the priestly office speaks to us of the saints who are engaged in ministering to God and therefore have a special part with Him.

We are, of course, not considering what is the official position of an ordained priest in an ecclesiastical system, for there are no garments mentioned here. We are, however, concerned with those who are called to be believer-priests. So the real question involves what really enters into the heart and mind of a believer who is called to proclaim "the unsearchable riches of Christ" and who has the ministry of reconciliation.

This ministry of reconciliation is a very responsible apostolic commission. What an office this is! It is an office just like that of the Savior, for as the Father has sent the Son, so He sends us with this ministry. "And all things are of God, who hath reconciled us to himself by Jesus Christ, and hath given to us the ministry of reconciliation" (2 Cor. 5:18).

This does not imply that we are mediators or saviors as the Lord himself is, but we are given the resources with which to point sinners to the Savior who delivers from sin and who intercedes before a holy God.

The believer-priest needs much spiritual sustenance of the quality that will fill his heart with a deep appreciation of God. This will ensure that His holy desires will be met, and that His people would learn to value these very features in the Lord Jesus.

Peter calls on believers to "follow his [Christ's] steps" (1 Pet. 2:21); and as we consider His steps we see that He never once went back. All His steps revealed the strength of the ox and the dignity of the goat as He moved in personal devotion to the will of God and to His Father's delight.

Feeding on the correct food, based on the whole Word of God, rightly divided, will strengthen us in the priestly feelings and energy so that our appreciation of redemptive work will deepen. God has never envisaged His people, as priests, growing feeble and impoverished. He has called us to himself with the intention that we should have every source of power available at our disposal and we, as children of God and believer-priests, should be marked by spiritual energy.

This spiritual energy and vitality was one of the great features which was evident in the early church, for it showed forth the essential freshness and life of God's service and pleasure. We have seen much spiritual decline since those remarkable days when the Holy Spirit moved with such liberty among the saints with signs following, and when the authority of Christ as head of His church was fully acknowledged.

Church history has shown that spiritual decline usually coincides with the setting up of a system of empty formalism which has affected our order of worship, stifled our freedom and quenched the Holy Spirit. There is a form of clericalism which only results in a dead atmosphere where the Lord's authority is usurped and where its church members are encouraged to obey the voice of man rather than the voice of God. No wonder we are told that God will spew such out of His mouth, as if to say that He is sickened by this presumption that man can rob Him of His glory and escape His judgment.

In our present-day Christianity, we see much that is only man-made. This is typical of the conditions recorded in Genesis 11 where we have an account of man's presumption when he sought to defy God. Here were mere earth-dwellers, seeking each other's cooperation, trying to promote an earthly unity which will increase their own fame and augment their own reputation. This is the germ which gives birth to earthly empires and unholy combinations, for they seek to deprive God of His glory as they say, "Go to"—which suggests haste and urgency. They are seen to be busy all the time. This is how the enemies of God have worked in all generations, by substituting the artificial for the natural. This is how the devil always has his counterfeit. They say, "Let us make bricks and burn them thoroughly," showing how they will use their own homemade materials to build their world, using bricks for stone and slime for mortar.

Man's religion is after the flesh today, and, as we look at it along with man's civilization, man's legal systems, man's social customs and activities, we find that they are built on the ideas and opinions of men, without any divine revelation. We thus find that man has built for himself a busy, active and miserable world.

Furthermore, he not only substitutes his own handmade bricks for God's stones, but he uses the slime of his own sinfulness instead of the mortar of faith in God, and the slime of sin instead of the love which binds the redeemed together.

Babylon is not built on stone or rock, for there is nothing of Christ in it. It is built on brick which is the product of man's own handiwork. Its builders have rejected the stone and take no account of living stones who are kindred with Christ, the Rock. Babylon is too busy making bricks which are sharpened and hardened to serve the same purpose as stone. But no amount of shaping will ever make sinful man, in his natural self, suitable for God's building. Natural man can only be shaped for Babel, but there is nothing of the Lord there. There is no divine material in Babel. It is a great religious structure with nothing of Christ in it.

The sinners' society can be a very united one, but its unity is in the bonds of false religion, a counterfeit Christianity without Christ. They are united by a common aggressive purpose or by filthy mirth, producing unclean things and unholy communications.

Only God can build the true city which has foundations of himself. The New Jerusalem is that city and it consists of the redeemed. It is the only happy society foreknown by the Father, purchased by the Son and called by the Holy Spirit. On the other hand, Babylon began to build in Christendom by turning her back on the true light. Christ's coming is therefore forgotten and the professors of Christianity become mere earth-dwellers who are concerned only in making a great name for themselves. So they decide to build a city and a tower, to create a memorial and have a constant monument lest they might be forgotten.

Here we see the principle of confederacy, for man knows that he cannot work in isolation in order to make an alternative to a city and place where God would place His name. This is the spirit of defiance of Babel that has existed ever since the Genesis 11 account.

Without the gospel we have Babylon. It is a city built to glorify man, but the true church glorifies God. How noisy it is for man to take the holiest things and make them contribute to his own glory; and who but God could give us such a history of the world of man's glory from Genesis 11 to the Revelation and show of its eventual overthrow.

When Israel failed, God gave the government to the Gentiles. He tried Babylon and gave absolute power to Nebuchadnezzar, but this king claimed the glory for himself. He says, "Is not this great Babylon, that I have built for the house of the kingdom by the might of *my* power, and for the honour of *my* majesty?" (Dan. 4:30, italics mine).

The Revelation shows Babylon at its very worst, like Belshazzar using the gold and silver vessels for his own idolatrous feast while the writing was already on the wall.

God has mercifully broken up the world's history. He has divided men, and given them opposing loyalties in the religious, political and social world, so that they can never destroy the power of the gospel. No wonder the place where the people sought to build the tower is called Babel. It has two meanings. In the Aramaic it means the gate of God, while in the Hebrew it means confusion. It is not beyond our reasoning powers to see that what the heathen may regard as the gate of God is only confusion in the sight of the godly.

The same is true of modern Babylon, which is the Greek word for Babel. Religious systems of our day may appear to be the very gate of God, but to the born-again Christian, they are

125

only confusion.

How different Babel is from the spiritual church in which they had holy unity and spoke the same language. In the spiritual church, they each went to their own company and "had all things common" (Acts 2:44). Here, then, was a company where sympathy and understanding was found. They were a praying company and spoke the Word of God with boldness.

The Old Testament shows us in type how hearts that are responsive towards God will provide a due portion to Him and His own; where there is an outflow of holy praise and worship to Him, there is that which will strengthen our priestly feelings and affections for Him and His own. The thought of Christ being the head of His church is very valuable and precious to those who believe. We achieve even greater heights when we consider the things that are for God, and can lay hold on what is conveyed to us as we think of God's inheritance. When we come to this, we can show the true priestly features in our Christian walk in such a way as will answer to His pleasure. Our declaration will not just be, "I am satisfied with Jesus," but "Is Jesus satisfied with me?"

With Him as our Lord and the Holy Spirit to give us power of witness, we shall be capable of shouldering our responsibility until the day when the government shall be on His shoulders and we will be with Him for all eternity.

We thus have reference to the shoulder, in Deuteronomy 18:3, which speaks to us of power and strength. It reminds us of the holy and energetic walk of the Lord Jesus in His devotion to the will of God. The gospels abound with impressions concerning His pathway which was in the strength of the ox and the humility of the sheep. We also see how His life of ministry is likewise appreciated by those who have the same priestly features.

126

## Priestly Features

Since the fall man has been marked by much weakness and is continually slipping and stumbling, but the Lord always makes provision for his recovery and way back. He has also equipped us with the necessary discernment and ability for spiritual judgment.

Chapter 18 of Deuteronomy, therefore, brings before us the portions of the priests and Levites, and we have a constant reminder of that prophet whom God would raise up in Israel. We, as believer-priests, have a part with God and share God's inheritance which is given to the redeemed in Christ.

Eternal life is a precious gift of God to sinful man, and out of the wealth of our inheritance we are able to minister to God's pleasure. If we are able to take on the right priestly features we will have the ability to appreciate and appropriate what is for God.

The priests' portions are the shoulder, the cheeks (or jawbones) and the maw (stomach).

The shoulder is really part of the arm, and this suggests the strength and power of God to deliver with an outstretched arm (Exod. 6:6). The redemption of the people of Israel from the bondage of Egypt was typical of the eternal redemption which was brought about by Christ. To redeem means to set free at a price. In Exodus, the price was the Egyptian first-born and the blood of the Passover lambs. The price of our redemption is the precious blood of Christ who was the Lamb without spot or blemish. He redeemed us from the curse of the law—He gave himself for us that He might redeem us from iniquity. This was done with an outstretched arm and with good judgments, for God's arm was extended to smite the Lord Jesus on Calvary, and thus destroy the power of the enemy. That same arm was also stretched out to deliver Him from death and gloriously raise Him from the grave. The great judgments needed for our redemption were poured out upon Christ, on whom fell all the waves and bellows of God's wrath.

We note that the cheeks (or jawbones) are a part of the priests' portion, and are reminded of the principle of mastication and meditation as typified in the clean creatures who chew the cud. No matter how rich the pasture may be, the function of the jawbones is to help obtain the proper nourishment. There is much literature available for believers and much produced by spiritual souls to the glory of God, but it is only as we appropriate what we have available that we are strengthened. It is never sufficient to be content just to hear things, or even to memorize them, but we should be concerned that we understand the spiritual importance of what the meanings really are.

Commentaries can be very helpful in our studies. However, we should always beware lest we allow them to be our master and lead us to believe what others have said about the Word of God rather than what the Word says for itself. All we say and believe should be tested by the Word itself and all we find in commentaries should be subjected to the light of the truth of the whole Word of God. This unchangeable truth should always be our critic, teacher and guide. We can never be approved of God unless we are prepared to search the Scriptures and see whether we are acting or speaking according to the inspired Word. We must always be ready and willing to prove all things so that we need not be ashamed of the truth.

Divine things have to be apprehended and as we masticate our spiritual food we find that we shall delight in the laws of the Lord.

Jesus, as a boy, was not just a passive observer or listener. He listened to his elders and asked questions. He took an active interest in the things He heard and all Scripture was food for Him. Likewise, we need intelligent and active exercise as we masticate the abundant supply of food.

Paul's appeal to Timothy is, "Meditate upon these things" (1 Tim. 4:15). In other words, we should consider the truth as it is presented to us. We should go into every detail, weigh every matter intelligently and see whether these things are so.

Let us consider what the apostle has to say, for "ye have an unction from the Holy One and ye know all things" (1 John 2:20) and "ye need not that any man teach you" (1 John 2:27). Remember how Jeremiah said that he not only ate the words, but that they were also a joy to him (15:16). His father had discovered the book of law among some rubbish and he became interested enough to read it and give himself to the understanding of it. From thence, holy feelings developed in his heart and he yearned for more knowledge of God. Truly, the Bereans were marked, in a spiritual sense, by using their "jawbones" as they diligently searched the Word of God to see whether all they heard matched with the Bible's teaching (Acts 17:11). The result was that many believed unto salvation and they proved that they were more noble than those of other parts.

The maw, or stomach, was also reserved for the priest and again we are reminded of the inward feelings and thoughts which characterized the Lord Jesus during His earthly ministry. God was always before Him and He had an endless supply of wisdom and intelligence to carry out the Father's desire. We have not only to listen to the truth and chew it over again and again, but we need to ponder it and receive it into our being so that we may show evidence that we have a living witness of the truth itself. It involves more than a merely outward show of behavior, but the very constitution and essence of our inner selves.

So, while the jawbones suggest mastication, the maw involves assimilation and this is what forms us and produces growth.

In a day when mere profession is widespread and there is such lack of spiritual substance among some professing Christians, we see how important it is that the food we take in should affect our constitution.

Various foods came into view as the children of Israel prepared to go into their inheritance, for they were told to prepare victuals for themselves as they were to pass over the Jordan in three days. The victuals would be strong meat and would correspond to the way in which Christ is presented to us in all His glory. He is the head of the body and over all principality and authority. His glories are largely based upon what He is rather than what He has done, and we need to set our minds on things above so that our lives are hid with Christ in God (Col. 3:2, 3). He regards His own redeemed as elect of God, for Paul tells us that we are holy and beloved.

If we break our links with the world by identification of ourselves with Christ in His death, He becomes our treasure and our links with one another become most precious.

# 16

# Take, Eat

We have seen how we may be helped in our consideration of spiritual food and how we may become Christ-like. Also how food is presented in the Word of God with the thought of building up our constitution, for food is supplied to man in order that he might live and be sustained.

Spiritually, the Lord's Supper provides us with the most distinguished food of all for here we have a direct reference to Christ himself. All other foods are typical, but at the Lord's table we are provided with Christ who is in our midst.

Light can be received but we can move in the light without faith. Light in itself is, therefore, not sufficient for there is indeed much light available but many are not satisfied. The mind can be affected by the light, but we need to be affected in our hearts. Food not only enters into the mouth, but it goes into the stomach and sustains us.

The gospels have much to say to us on this very line and John, particularly, points out that light comes to us and brings in life. But life has to be sustained. Christ came to do the will of Him that sent Him. His meat was to please the Father and this same meat is also essential for us in our Christian walk and testimony.

Divine principles always govern the position of the saints. When the Lord's people meet together we act upon a principle, but we also need spiritual sustenance. We, therefore, have in view a company meeting together, governed by principles and sustained by the right kind of spiritual food which alone will bring out those features which conform to Christ.

When we eat, we are showing that we appreciate the very things we consume. By partaking of the Lord's Supper, we are testifying that we are lovers of Christ and want to be like Him. Colossians speaks of Christ being in the saints, "Christ in you" (1:27). He would be seen in us and we desire to be like Him, both collectively and individually. The more we are like Him individually, the more we will be like Him as a company, and there will be evidence that Christ is in us.

When the Lord said to Saul on the Damascus Road, "I am Jesus whom thou persecutest" (Acts 9:5), He was obviously referring to himself as living in the saints. In the same way we should be able to see Christ in our brethren and sisters, and those who have been on the pilgrim path for many years should become more Christ-like than younger Christians. The old man is to disappear, although this may take a long time. This putting off of the old man in us is an act which involves decrease. John the Baptist said that he must decrease and Christ must increase (John 3:30). When Christ himself increases in His people, they become attractive and thus invite Satan's opposition and attacks. We may not see what he is doing; but he will be busy, even taking on the form of an angel of light. He has his own way of getting at us and will publicly seize what belongs to Christ and pervert its true meaning.

The Old Testament manna was for every day and we need to meet its conditions in the wilderness. It speaks of Christ meeting our need in the wilderness. It speaks of Christ meeting our need in adverse circumstances. Young converts need this manna as they move in the world among worldly people. They need the right kind of food to strengthen them and those of us who are elders need to provide it for them. They also need the right kind of spiritual refreshment, for the flesh never changes and it will rise at a time when the enemy of our souls can use it to the best advantage.

Matthew 26 tells us about the institution of the Lord's Supper. It was the Feast of Unleavened Bread. What we are taking in spiritually will keep us transparent and pure as we put what we learn into practice. The right food will bring out the positive condition in us so that we become truthful and transparent with each other so that we would not be vague about important things. We will always be sure and certain about the things we are saying and thinking so that our "yea" will always be "yea" and our "nay" will be "nay." When the Lord himself said, "Take, eat; this is my body" (Matt. 26:26), He made a very positive statement which demands of us that we eat the bread of sincerity and truth. When we take a positive stand we then receive power and energy to move as saints, becoming like Christ. If we are sincere, truthful and transparent, our brethren will have confidence in us.

We are therefore told that having taken the bread and blessed it, he broke it and gave to the disciples and said, "Take, eat." We are led to have love for all the saints, and everything that belongs to Christ, we learn to love. We learn to take account of His body and how He suffered, bled and died for our redemption. This should stir us up so that we desire to know more of Him, not as a dead Christ, but as a living Lord.

As we become more exercised regarding the breaking of bread at the Lord's table, we enter more into the real gain of the Lord's death. This can be very humbling for the truth is always bitter.

The Revelation is, of course, prophetic, and in chapter 10 it is stating that what enters into our inward parts will not remain the same as it was in our mouth. It may be bitter to the taste, but it may also be very profitable. On the other hand, we may be attracted to the sweetness of a lovely song or a nice word of ministry, but this can change when it is assimilated into our being.

The people may cry, "Prophesy unto us smooth things." We may be tempted to say nice things to our hearers for that is what they want. But if we are going to bring in that which is of God's mind, we may have to prescribe a bitter pill.

John is told to go and take the little book that was opened in the hand of the angel which had come down from heaven, clothed with a cloud, and whose countenance was as the sun. The angel's feet were as pillars of fire and he set his right foot on the sea and his left foot on the earth. Here we see two great spheres of influence, and the Lord is in full control of both for he has a foot on each. So, although outwardly, the public testimony may appear fragmented and deteriorated, we know that the Lord is in full control. This should comfort our hearts in a day when we see the increase of secular powers making way for the beast.

John eats the book and it becomes sweet in his mouth, but when it reaches his stomach it is bitter. The truth must reach our affections. We are oftentimes reminded that Christ loves the saints as they correspond to himself as they have fellowship in His own sufferings. He also had the joy and the sweetness of fellowship before Him as He endured the bitterness of the cross. This is why the wine which we all drink at the Lord's table is both bitter and sweet.

At Jericho, the men told Elisha that the situation was good but the water was bad (2 Kings 2:19). Things may appear all

134

right, but the water must also be pure. Salt was put in and the water was purified, providing a good supply for the city; for salt in itself is purifying, though perhaps bitter to the taste.

We have also a most attractive reference to food in the Word of God when we consider the tree of life. This is brought to our notice as early as Genesis 2 and is again laid before us in Revelation 2 and 22. It is a remarkable thing that this feature should begin so early in man's history and yet should be mentioned again at the consummation of God's ways.

The tree of life is said to be "in the midst of the garden" (Gen. 2:9), and likewise we have the tree of the knowledge of good and evil in the same verse. Truly, God purposed that man should enjoy life, and the tree of life was the central thought in His mind. But man did not partake of it before the Fall of Man and it was guarded in case man should live forever in a dishonoring condition after the Fall. God, in His mercy, decreed that man must die and thus He ensured that man would not be an eternal burden to himself.

The tree of life is a promise of life before the Fall and an evidence that the whole sin question had been raised in God's universe even before the creation of man. Christ is the tree of life and we are told that "The trees of the LORD are full of sap" (Psa. 104:16). In the future world, Christ will be one with His own; and God's desire is that we should have an eye of faith which perceives His Son.

As the tree of life, Christ came that we might have life and have it more abundantly (John 10:10). In Him was life (John 1:4). He is the life (John 14:6). In His death, He gave us flesh to eat which is of himself; and whoever takes advantage of this death, by receiving and assimilating the gift of Christ himself, coming to Him in simple faith, enters into eternal life. We are then able to walk by faith in the paradise and feed on the tree of life. The only condition is that we wash our robes (Rev. 7:14).

As the tree of life was in the midst of the garden, so the Lord Jesus Christ is in the midst of His own. He lives in our lives and hearts and is the center of the coming glory, the source of all joy and our everlasting solution to the question of good and evil. God is never thwarted by Satan's power or the Fall of Man; and we can stand, through faith in the value of Calvary, rejoicing that grace now reigns through righteousness unto eternal life.

It is often said that when we come to Christ and are born again we are placed in a position that is as if we had never sinned. In other words we are regarded as innocent. There is, however, more virtue in the death of Christ than that, for as we feed on Him as the tree of life we are set before God in divine righteousness. We thus find that the enemy is defeated, God is glorified, and we are free to enjoy the blessings of eternal life.

In Revelation 22, the tree of life is in the midst of the street, and of the river, on this side and on that side. The river, as in Genesis, is associated with the tree and this suggests refreshment.

As we meditate upon the triumph of God in finding a solution to the question of good and evil, our hearts are drawn out to the Lord Jesus Christ himself. We can feed on Him as the tree of life, producing fruit and perpetual freshness. How precious is this triumph, and how wonderful is the way in which Christ brings us to the rest in His love and to enjoy the life which He has given us.

We also see that there is only one street and yet the tree is there, showing us the blessedness of the saints meeting together in liberty and freedom, enjoying the overcoming life in all its richness.

The leaves of the tree are for the healing of the nations which are so wounded and torn. How different will the nations be when the leaves have been applied so that there will be no

136

more discontent, envy, jealousy and strife. What a prospect awaits those who call on the name of the Lord for they will enjoy God's ordering of things and will learn war no more. Wherever God's grace is appropriated there is holy movement and power for the healing of wounds and sores, for there shall be no more curse and no more night.

There was no need of healing in Genesis for the tree of life was revealed before sin came in; but now we find that Christ is the only source of everlasting satisfaction to every soul that feeds upon Him. His grace alone applies the healing balm to the nations of the world. The day will come when nations will see that Christ alone can bring blessing and that He will not only shake them but will be their desire. May our hearts feed on Christ as the tree of life, enjoy all the precious fruits and drink of the river which makes glad the city of God so that we may sing:

> Lord, in Thee we taste the sweetness
> of the Tree of Life above
> Taste its own eternal meetness
> For the heavenly land we love.
>
> In eternal counsels purposed
> Food of heavenly life to be;
> Fresh and ever new are yielded
> Fruits of life on that blest Tree.

(J.N. Darby)